The Parks
of
Washington

by
Nicky Leach

SIERRA PRESS
MARIPOSA, CA

DEDICATION

This book is dedicated to the prolific late Northwest poet William Stafford. He once said: "Anyone actually doing art needs to maintain this knack for responding to the immediate, the region; for that's where the art is." His poetry powerfully evokes the Pacific Northwest for me and continues to influence my own writing about western landscapes.

> Pines embraced by scarves of snow
> wait for the sun.
> Hemlocks repeat their millions of prayers
> bowed down.
>
> Deep in its den a sleepy bear
> sucks its paw
> where the dream of the forest unfolds in the
>   mountains
> on and on.
>
> Out there in a lake a wilderness eye
> opens to shine
> while stars walk west on their endless hunt
> for their perfect home.
>
> Whoever you are, you live in that arch;
> you belong,
> one of the lost but surrounded by prayer-trees,
> all alone.

—from *The Long Sigh the Wind Makes*

INSIDE FRONT COVER
Post-sunset glow, Ruby Beach, Olympic National Park. PHOTO ©ALAN MAJCHROWICZ
PAGE 2
Sunset, Second Beach, Olympic National Park. PHOTO ©JEFF D. NICHOLAS
TITLE PAGE
Foggy morning along Ennis Creek, Olympic National Park. PHOTO ©STEVE TERRILL
PAGE 4 (BELOW)
Sub-alpine wildflowers, Mount Rainier National Park. PHOTO ©TERRY DONNELLY
PAGE 4/5
Eruption of March 8, 2005, Mount St. Helens National Volcanic Monument. PHOTO ©TYSON FISHER

CONTENTS

PAGE 6/7
Evening clouds over Mount Shuksan, North Cascades National Park seen from Mount Baker–Snoqualmie National Forest. PHOTO ©TERRY DONNELLY
PAGE 7 (BELOW)
Balsamroot at Gov. Tom McCall Nature Preserve, Columbia River National Scenic Area.
PHOTO ©TERRY DONNELLY

7

WASHINGTON STATE

Mount Rainier above the fog. PHOTO ©LARRY CARVER

It's a hot, dry August afternoon at Mount St. Helens National Volcanic Monument in southern Washington State. The parking lot of Johnston Ridge Observatory, the closest viewpoint to Mount St. Helens on Scenic Spirit Lake Highway 504, is almost full. Just 5 miles away, the enormous northside crater created by the eruption of the volcano on May 18, 1980, presides over the ghostly ash-gray landscape of the blast zone. It is a moonscape of stream-carved pumice plain, redirected rivers and lakes, and remnant blowdown forest strewn like matchsticks on a nearby ridge.

News footage of the blast—one of many in Mount St. Helens' violent 40,000-year history—cannot prepare you for the scene. The raw energy of the mountain is palpable, even 25 years later. There is no soothing green forest, no Fuji-like snowy peak, no canoes on an alpine mountain lake, nothing comforting at all, in fact. This is a land in the midst of rebirth—and like all births, the scene is messy, complicated, primordial, awe-inspiring.

Since 1980, Mount St. Helens has been the climax of any trip to Washington's national parks and monuments, simply because it demonstrates just what can happen in an active range like the Cascade Mountains on the growing western edge of a very young continent. Mount St. Helens is the most active of a string of volcanoes along the Pacific Northwest coast, which also includes nearby Mount Adams, Mount Rainier, Glacier Peak, and Mount Baker in Washington, and to the south, Mount Hood in Oregon and Lassen Peak and Mount Shasta in northern California.

The Most Dangerous Volcano in the Cascades award, though, goes to 14,410-ft. Mount Rainier, a mountain so high that it makes it own weather. Rainier's 25 glaciers—the most of any single peak in the lower 48 states—are also its greatest liability: even small eruptions have historically triggered massive mud-flows that would seriously impact modernday communities. Visible for 100 miles in any direction, it's hard to believe that Mount Rainier's distinctive form could in any way change.

A national park since 1899, *Tahoma*, or "The Mountain," as it was known to the local Puget Sound Indian tribes, exerts a magnetic appeal, an almost other-worldly presence on a clear day brooding over the metropolitan areas of Seattle and Tacoma. Its roads, historic districts, legendary forests, glaciers, and still-steaming summit craters attract some two million visitors a year, from scenic drivers, campers, and hikers to the 10,000 climbers who try to reach the top of The Mountain.

By comparison, North Cascades National Park Service Complex, beginning northeast of Seattle and extending to the US-Canada border, is relatively unvisited, with only 450,000 visitors a year. The jagged range, sculpted into distinctive knifelike peaks by glaciation, is mostly unexplored. The main access for short hikes as well as long climbs is the highly popular North Cascades Scenic Highway, which links the wetter Pacific side of the mountains and the drier Methow valley in the east-side rain shadow, via State Route 20.

Set aside in 1968 after a long fight by local conservation-ists, the complex also includes Ross Lake National Recreation Area, three man-made reservoirs backed up by three hydroelectric dams on the Skagit River, and Lake Chelan National Recreation Area, a natural lake basin deepened by a predecessor of one of the park's 312 glaciers, the largest number of glaciers of any park in the Lower 48. The North Cascades are primarily nonvolcanic mountains, composed of rocks rafted onto the early northwestern continent and uplifted. Glacier Peak and Mount Baker volcanoes lie just outside the boundaries of the national park.

Washington's third national park—Olympic—owes more to the ocean than to the land. The park is located on a large bearpaw-shaped peninsula, bordered on three sides by the Strait of Juan de Fuca, Hood Canal, and the Pacific Ocean. Its high moun-tains are composed of basalts (hardened volcanic lava) and sand-stone and shale sediments that formed on the ocean floor. Geolo-gists theorize that the submarine sediments rode east on the continental plate and jammed beneath the basalts, elevating the Olympic Mountains 10 to 20 million years ago. Ice-age glaciers helped carve the Strait of Juan de Fuca and Puget Sound, separat-ing the Olympics from nearby lands. The peninsula's dense forests of Douglas fir, western hemlock, western redcedar, and Pacific

OPPOSITE: Mount St. Helens seen from Johnston Ridge, late afternoon. PHOTO ©JOHN MARSHALL

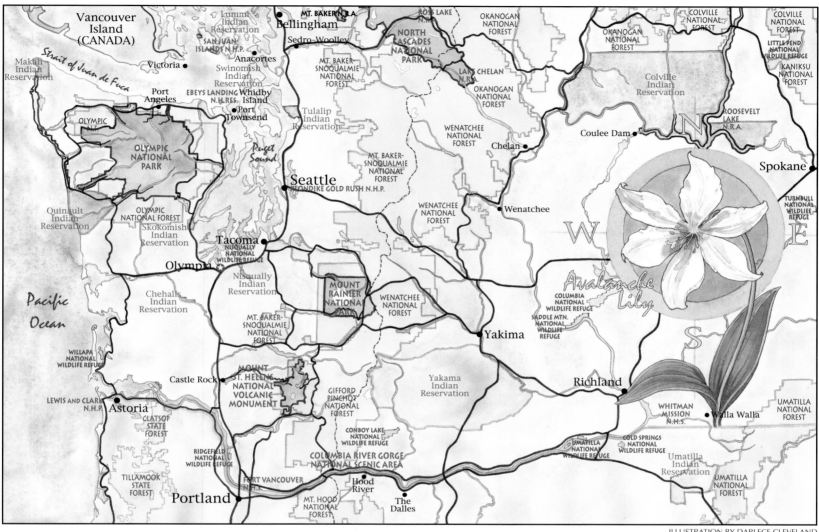

ILLUSTRATION BY DARLECE CLEVELAND

Washington is 68,139 square miles in area and is in the Pacific Northwest, the coastal region that also includes Oregon, northern California, and southeast Alaska. It is known as the Evergreen State in honor of the old-growth forests made possible by the ample rainfall that falls on the coastal region. Two towering mountain ranges—the mainland Cascades and the Olympics—are responsible for Washington's famous weather. The climate veers between very wet—160-200 inches of annual rainfall along the crest of the Olympic Mountains—and very dry—less than 15 inches east of the Cascades, semi-desert.

Washington's major federal lands—Mount Rainier, North Cascades, and Olympic National Parks; Mount St. Helens National Volcanic Monument; and Columbia Gorge National Scenic Area—all display these Jekyll and Hyde weather conditions, which are also responsible for the remarkable biodiversity found within their large areas.

Water—too much or too little—has long characterized the natural landscape here. The Channeled Scablands, bordering the Columbia River east of the Cascades, were carved by Ice Age floods then left high and dry as the climate warmed. Today, the Columbia River is a managed waterway through its series of dams that helped revolutionize the economy of the Pacific Northwest in the 20th century.

Seattle, one of the most beautiful waterfront cities in the world, is the cultural center of western Washington, and within three hours of all the parks in this book. To the west are 80-mile-long Puget Sound, the Strait of Juan de Fuca, and Hood Canal; to the east are Lakes Washington and Sammamish; to the northeast, Lakes Ross and Chelan. Puget Sound is a deep fjord carved by the mile-thick Vashon glacier during the last Ice Age. It's home to Pacific harbor seals, orcas, salmon, bald eagles, and other wildlife. Thickly forested islands dot the Sound and include such popular destinations as Bainbridge, Vashon, and Whidbey Islands, as well as the San Juan Islands.

Bridges span bodies of water and help connect this deeply glaciated region. Interstate 90 transects the state, leaving Seattle, crossing Lake Washington via Mercer Island, and continuing over Snoqualmie Pass, an old Indian route spanning the Central Cascades. Interstate 5, Washington's main north-south route, passes through Seattle north to Vancouver, British Columbia, and is the main access to Mount St. Helens, Mount Rainier, and the North Cascades Highway. US 101, the coastal route from California, circles the Olympic Peninsula and crosses the mouth of the Columbia River before heading south through Oregon. Interstate 84, the main freeway through the Columbia Gorge, is on the Oregon side. Washington's excellent car ferry system connects the mainland, the islands, and the Olympic Peninsula, and, for many, is the only way to travel in the Northwest.

Fire and ice. All five of the federally managed units in this book are geological parks that, in some way, owe their existence to volcanism and glaciation. Despite the dense vegetation in the low elevations—the result of Washington's record-setting rainfall—the high peaks that tower over this landscape beyond treeline are rocky places, subject to grinding ice, which has left behind tortured pinnacles, wide river valleys filled with boulders and debris, and alpine lakes that reflect the distinctive summits around them.

CONTINENTAL DECONSTRUCTION

According to plate tectonic theory, proven by post-war technological advances, the earth is made up of separate continental plates and oceanic plates. They are composed largely of granite, soft sedimentary strata are transformed into hard metamorphic rock by extreme heat below the earth's surface, which melts and reconstitutes the rock. The outer layer of the earth's molten mantle, known as the lithosphere, is in fact quite thin. Crustal plates floating atop it move around on convection currents created by that heat, like sailboats on the ocean.

Early on in the earth's history, these plates were joined in a tesselated pattern, like pieces of a puzzle, to form the supercontinent Pangaea. The places where the plates meet are, not surprisingly, very unstable. Areas of weakness, known as faults, become places where movements deep within the earth can have dramatic effects on the surface, through seismic events such as earthquakes and volcanic eruptions.

Where plates grind past each other in a north-south direction, you'll find a transform boundary that carries along a section of one plate, such as the San Andreas Fault in California, which is gradually closing the gap between Los Angeles and San Francisco. In oceanic faults, plates pull away from each other, forming an oceanic ridge where magma from the earth's core escapes as volcanic eruptions, then cools in seawater, leaving behind pillow basalts. When oceanic and continental plates collide, the heavier oceanic plate will be forced beneath the lighter continental plate into a large trench that parallels the plate

boundary—a process known as subduction.

WASHINGTON DEBUTS

About a billion years ago, as Washington lay underwater, a new oceanic ridge formed. As it spread, the Pacific Ocean widened and Asia broke away from western America. Things remained pretty quiet on the western front for about 800 million years, though. The western coastline, now located about where the Idaho-Washington border is today, met a shallow ocean floor. Here, sediments built up on an offshore continental shelf and muddy rivers and streams braided to the ocean across a gentle, sandy coastal delta.

It wasn't until 200 million years ago, when the Atlantic oceanic ridge off the East Coast began to pull apart, widening the Atlantic and separating North America from Africa and Europe, that Washington made its first appearance. With both oceans spreading, the heavier Pacific plate was forced into a trench off the coast of eastern Washington. Sedimentary rocks buckled, forming the Kootenay Arc, and melted into a large granitic batholith that now underlies northeastern Washington and adjoining western Montana and Idaho.

Island continents floating in the ocean began to collide with North America, creating micro-continents attached to the mainland. The first of these was the Okanagan micro-continent, which joined northeastern Washington about 100 million years ago to become what is now the Okanagan Highlands. Washington grew again, 50 million years later, when the North Cascades micro-continent became part of North America. The Okanagan and Kootenay trenches were now replaced by a pre-existing trench west of the North Cascades micro-continent. These island-formed terranes, in large part, make up what we now know as Washington.

ANCESTRAL VOLCANOES

Starting 40 million years ago, eruptions built the early stratovolcanic cones of the Western Cascades, the precursors to the modern Cascades. Evidence of these early volcanic eruptions can be seen near Mount Rainier in the form of the Ohanapecosh and Stevens Ridge Formations and the more recent Tatoosh pluton, which underlies million-year-old Mount Rainier.

Interestingly, the volcanic eruptions

ABOVE: Moss-covered andesite columns, Mount Rainier National Park. PHOTO ©JOHN MARSHALL

that built the Columbia Plateau in eastern Washington began in between the time the ancient Western Cascades had snuffed out and before the modern Cascades appeared. Until 6-7 million years ago, the 1,200-mile-long Columbia River flowed to the south of its present course. But it was then repeatedly pushed northward by Yakima Basalt lava flows oozing a mile deep across a 50,000-square-mile area from northeastern Idaho.

A million years ago, the focus shifted back to the Cascades, with the pumice and lava eruptions that built Mount Rainier and later decapitated it by 2,000 feet. Mounts St. Helens, Hood, and Adams began to appear 70,000 years ago. Of the three, Mount St. Helens is the youngest and remains the most active. Further violent events like the May 1980 eruptions and subsequent mudflows that destroyed the perfect cone of the volcano are expected in the future.

THE OLYMPIC MOUNTAINS

Unrelated to the Cascade volcanoes, the 6,000-8,000-foot Olympics are crumpled sedimentary rocks contained within a horseshoe of harder Crescent Formation basalts, easily seen on the way to Hurricane Ridge in Olympic National Park. The basalts oozed up along the edge of the continental shelf about 50 million years ago, cooling on contact with the ocean into underwater mountains and islands of "pillow basalts." This new material was joined by marine and continental sediments, which shed into the ocean in such thick layers they eventually compressed into sandstone and shale strata.

Meanwhile, the mobile North American Plate collided with the expanding Pacific Plate, which subducted under the continent. In the vicinity of Vancouver Island,

where North America bends, the oceanic plate got hung up. Geologists still debate the origins of the Olympics. However, it's thought that the immense submerged delta of sandstone and shale formed farther out in the ocean rode back to the continent and jammed beneath the basalts, forcing the Olympics to rise from the sea 10 to 20 million years ago.

GLACIATION AND CATASTROPHIC FLOODS

The Olympics, Cascades, and most of modern Washington have been sculpted by glaciation, which began about 2 million years ago, when a cooling trend ushered in the last ice age. A succession of ice sheets moved south from Canada, covering the entire Puget Sound region. The most recent, the Vashon ice sheet carved out the troughs of Puget Sound, the Strait of Juan de Fuca, Hood Canal, and Lake Washington—leaving behind islands and glacial ice-melt sounds when the climate warmed

and the ice sheets receded 10,000 years ago.

On the highest peaks glaciers are permanent fixtures, ebbing and flowing from summer to winter with snow build-up in their own U-shaped valleys. The high country is filled with signs of glaciation: cirque lakes cupped into high mountainsides; knife-edged aretes forming ridgelines; house-sized boulders known as erratics stranded on hillsides; valley walls polished and striated by moving glaciers; icy meltwater in lakes; rivers cloudy with the ground-up rock known as glacial flour, and edged by gravels deposited by glaciers as lateral (side) moraines and terminal (end) moraines.

If volcanoes provided the raw material for today's Columbia Gorge, then floodwaters have been the master sculptors. At the end of the Ice Age, 19,000-12,000 years ago, a lobe of ice flowed up the canyon of Montana's Clark Fork River and formed a 2,000-foot-high ice dam that impounded 500 cubic miles of water in a lake dubbed glacial Lake Missoula. Melting ice water repeatedly breached the dam, sending ice- and boulder-filled floods across eastern Washington to carve the dry falls and coulees of today's Columbia Plateau.

The most damaging of this series of catastrophic floods (known as the Bretz Floods after the persistent scientist who first popularized what, in the 1930s, seemed an outlandish theory) carved the Columbia River Gorge. Floodwaters surged as high as 1,000 feet through Wallula Gap, buzzing vertically through basalts, sculpting channeled scabland terraces, and eventually leaving side canyons (coulees), waterfalls, boulders and gravels high and dry. The energy was equivalent, said geologist John Elliot Allen, to the explosion for 10 days of a hydrogen bomb every 36 minutes.

ABOVE: Emmons Glacier, Mount Rainier. PHOTO ©CHARLES GURCHE

In July 1996, two men watching boat races on the Columbia River near Kennewick stumbled upon a skeleton in the riverbank. When a local archaeologist investigated, he discovered an ancient arrowhead buried in the right hip of the male skeleton. He concluded the man was a paleo-Indian hunter who died 9,000 years ago.

Most interesting was the skull, which showed characteristics unlike modern American Indians. It's long been thought that the first people arrived in North America via the Bering Land Bridge between Mongolia and Alaska that opened up at the end of the Ice Age, 12,000 years ago. But recent discoveries of a 15,000-year-old site in South America and a 17,000-year-old spear point from southern France on the East Coast have changed things. Scientists now conjecture waves of migration, including long ocean voyages in coracle boats made of hides.

A row over the bones ensued. The Army Corps of Engineers contacted local Umatilla and other Indian tribes, as required by the 1990 Native American Graves and Repatriation Act (NAGPRA), designed to return native remains to affiliated tribes for reburial. Scientists argued in court that the find was too important to simply rebury without study. In a stalemate that lasted nine years, Kennewick Man was locked up at the University of Washington's Burke Museum in Seattle. Eventually a court cleared the way for scientists to study the skeleton in 2005. Preliminary findings suggest that he is indeed Native American, about 45 years old, 5 feet 9 inches, and lived 8,400 – 9,200 years ago, when the climate in eastern Washington was cooler and wetter.

Kennewick Man is the most recent of several Clovis-era sites discovered in Wash-

ington. A cave near Wenatchee yielded the jawbone of an arctic fox and forest animals found in cooler environments. Artifacts excavated from the Marmes Rock Shelter on the Upper Columbia River during dam construction in 1969 showed it had been used for millennia. In the 1970s, a farmer near Sequim, on the Olympic Peninsula, turned up ancient mastodon bones embedded with a spear point, and over a half-million extraordinary artifacts were excavated from a centuries-old Makah Indian

village buried in a mudslide.

NATIVE PARADISE

People in Washington adapted to the wet west side of the Cascade Mountains and the dry extremes of the Columbia Plateau in different ways. Beginning more than 6,000 years ago, spurred by the arrival of western red cedar trees that supported many cultural advances, existing western Washington tribes began to inhabit the mouths of rivers along the Pacific Coast, Puget Sound, and the Columbia River and its tributaries.

Snohomish and Hoh people utilized canoes made of cedar to travel along coastal waterways and lived in communal cedar longhouses. Social status was recognized through the potlatch, a ceremony that empha-

sized eating, dancing, and the redistribution of gifts, such as blankets and carved cedar boxes, by chiefs to prove their power and prestige.

Lowland forests yielded fruits, nuts, and roots. Shellfish could be readily gathered on the tidal flats. The elite in Makah villages were whale hunters who harpooned migrating gray whales from their huge dugout canoes. Record-sized salmon annually returned to their birthplaces in the rivers to spawn in such numbers it was said you could walk across their backs from one bank to the other. Fishermen used nets strung in streams and dipnets from high platforms on the Columbia River. Salmon was dried and smoked for future use and was the focal point of ceremonial life.

East of the Cascades, the Okanogan, Spokane, Wenatchee, Yakama, Cayuse, Nez Perce, and Palouse tribes also fished for salmon on the Columbia and its tributaries. In summer, they moved around, collecting roots and berries in hide "sally bags" that were later elaborately decorated with colorful trade beads. Skins were obtained by hunting inland mountain animals like elk, bison, bear, and deer. In summer, these hides covered portable tipis made of long poles; in winter, they roofed semisubterranean pithouses in the canyon bottoms. When the Spanish reintroduced horses to America, Columbia Plateau people traveled farther afield. Tribes from east and west Washington paddled up the Columbia to attend huge annual rendezvous near The Dalles to trade, socialize, and intermarry.

HISTORIC CHANGES

This pleasant way of life ended within a few years of contact with Europeans, who brought Old World diseases like smallpox that wiped

ABOVE: Ozette petroglyphs at Wedding Rocks, Olympic National Park. PHOTO ©FRED HIRSCHMANN

out New World tribes. In 1775, Spanish sailors Bruno Heceta and Juan de la Bodega y Quadra claimed Point Grenville in the name of the king of Spain and, three years later, Captain James Cook declared the Washington coast and what is now Vancouver Island for Britain. While the Spanish were absentee landlords, Britain moved strongly to take possession and monopolize natural resources. In 1792, Captain George Vancouver charted the Washington coast and Puget Sound, naming Vancouver Island, Mount Rainier, Mount Baker, Mount St. Helens, and Puget Sound for himself and other important officials.

That same year, American fur trader Robert Gray sailed into the mouth of the Columbia River and named it for his ship. Following the 800,000-square-mile Louisiana Purchase from France in 1803, U.S. President Thomas Jefferson appointed Captains Meriwether Lewis and William Clark to mount an expedition to survey the West. The mission of the 1804–1806 expedition was to seek a Northwest Passage connecting the coasts, learn about the plants and animals of the new lands, and make friendly contact with Native Americans.

THE OREGON COUNTRY

After Lewis and Clark's report was released, settlement of the Pacific Northwest moved rapidly. American fur trader John Jacob Astor built a post at Astoria, Oregon, at the mouth of Columbia. In 1824, John McLoughlin, factor of the powerful Hudson's Bay Company, countered with a new British trading post on the north bank of the Columbia River. The popular post was eventually abandoned to the United States, who took control of western lands in 1846 and built Fort Vancouver nearby.

In 1836, Dr. Marcus and Narcissa Whitman built a mission near Walla Walla and also found themselves hosting a tidal wave of wagon train settlers traveling the Oregon Trail. In 1847, in an act that shocked the nation, the Whitmans were massacred by several Cayuse Indians angry at the decimation of the tribe by smallpox.

Congress moved quickly to protect settlers by creating a new Washington Territory. Between 1854 and 1855, governor Isaac Stevens pressured Indian tribes to move off the Columbia River onto the inland Yakama, Colville, Umatilla, and Warm Springs reservations. Leaders agreed to sign the treaties on condition they retained fishing and hunting rights at their "usual and customary" places. These treaties have been upheld in court and guarantee tribes half the natural resources on their former lands.

THE MODERN ERA

Asians flooded into Washington to help construct the Northern Pacific Railroad, which reached Puget Sound in 1883. In 1888, Washington became the 42nd state in the union, and Olympia, at the mouth of the Nisqually River, the new capital. Logging, mining, fishing, and eventually agriculture found ready markets back east, and Seattle, Spokane, and Tacoma grew up as processing and transportation centers. Between 1897 and 1908, Seattle supplied Yukon gold rush miners who arrived via railroad then traveled by boat up Alaska's Inside Passage. Trade with Alaska and East Asia also spurred shipbuilding.

As the cities grew crowded, westside residents increasingly traveled to the Cascade and Olympic mountains to hike, climb, ski, and enjoy the clean air of the mountains. They were inspired by early adventurers like Theodore Winthrop whose book *The Canoe and the Saddle* recorded his 1853 paddle journey across Puget Sound and exploration of the east slopes of Mount Rainier, where a glacier is now named for him.

In the 1930s, dams were built on the Columbia River under President Franklin Roosevelt's New Deal. They provided jobs during the Depression and engineered the river for navigation, flood control, irrigation to eastern Washington farms, and hydroelectric power. Even as the dams contributed to destroying the annual salmon runs on the rivers, cheap electricity allowed Seattle to prosper and turned southeastern Washington's Palouse Hills into the most productive agricultural area in the country. An aluminum factory supplied aircraft manufacturer Boeing in World War II and helped it grow into a major post-war industry.

In the 1980s, Seattle underwent another Industrial Revolution, this time in high-tech, when software giant Microsoft was founded on the eastern shore of Lake Washington. In 2000, the metropolitan area had 3.6 million residents, all living within a few hours of some of the most dramatic national parks in the nation.

ABOVE: Bonneville Dam on the Columbia River. PHOTO ©JEFFREY L. TORRETTA

Meriwether Lewis, a Virginia-born frontiersman and army captain, served as President Thomas Jefferson's secretary before being hand-picked by Jefferson to lead the expedition that would make him famous. He chose William Clark, an old army comrade, as his second-in-command. Congress appropriated $2,500 for supplies. The largest single budget item was for red flannel, pocket mirrors, beads, fishhooks, and needles to offer as gifts to Indians en route.

The Corps of Discovery, as they were popularly known, set out in May 1804 from Camp Wood, Missouri, and numbered 25 people, among them Clark's African-American slave Ben York, considered "great medicine" by the Indians he encountered. In the winter of 1804, the expedition wintered at Fort Mandan, North Dakota, and invited trapper Jean Baptiste Charboneau and his captive Shoshone wife Sacagawea and son Pompey to join them the following spring. Sacagawea's knowledge of plants and animals, the

country between Fort Mandan and the Rockies, and family connections proved invaluable in the unknown lands to the west.

The weary expedition arrived in Washington on October 10, 1805, and was welcomed by Nez Perce Chief Timothy in his tribe's large settlement at the mouth of the Snake River. The party continued following the Snake west, passing the mouth of the Palouse River, and eventually reached the Columbia on October 16. As they journeyed toward the Pacific, they encountered River People fishing for chinook at the height of the fall salmon harvest. They astonished local Indians by successfully rafting Celilo Falls near The Dalles but portaged around the Cascades (Great Falls) at Cascade Locks, Oregon. The expedition camped near a large volcanic mass next to the river, which Clark named Beacon Rock.

Their first sight of the ocean came on November 7. As the weather worsened, they continued exploring the coastline around Cape Dis-

appointment, Washington, named by British captain John Meares in 1788, after he missed the entrance to the Columbia River. With winter coming on hard, they built a wooden stockade fort at Fort Clatsop, Oregon. The expedition endured 100 days of rain while waiting to make the return trip. They set out in April and arrived back in Washington D.C. in September 1806.

Fort Clatsop and Fort Canby are two of the final 17 sites in Washington and Oregon on the 3,750-mile Lewis and Clark National Historical Trail. Both have excellent visitor centers and were featured prominently in celebrations marking the 200th anniversary of the 1804–1806 expedition in 2005. Sadly, the 1955 replica of the stockade at Fort Clatsop burned down a month before the bicentennial. Plans are underway to rebuild it.

ABOVE: Lighthouse at Cape Disappointment. PHOTO ©STEVE TERRILL   **OPPOSITE:** Columbia River and Vista House at Crown Point from Chanticleer Point. PHOTO ©PAT O'HARA

Lenticular cloud hovering over Mount Rainier. PHOTO ©RON WARFIELD

MOUNT RAINIER

"Of all the fire mountains which, like beacons, once blazed along the Pacific Coast," wrote famed environmentalist and mountain lover John Muir in the *Atlantic Monthly*, "Mount Rainier is the noblest in form, has the most interesting forest cover, and . . . is the highest and most flowery. . . . [It] should be made a national park and guarded while yet its bloom is on."

That bloom, in the subalpine meadows above Paradise, on the southwest side of Mount Rainier, is what is drawing thousands of admirers this balmy sunny day. The yellow glacier lilies poking through spring snowfields are long gone. In their place are broad, grassy swales filled with wildflowers. They soften the craggy face of the mountain with lazy drifts of purple lupine, scarlet Indian paintbrush, penstemon, and the tough but fragile pink heather I associate with the northern moors of my native England.

Saghalie Illahe, "Heavenly Place" or "Land of Peace," is the Salish Indian name for these spectacular wildflower meadows, which Muir called "Gardens of Eden." The current name, Paradise, bestowed by a member of the Longmire family in 1885, is equally lofty. It's a symbol of the sacredness of this mountain for the 2 million visitors that come here annually, and the 3.6 million people who look at it every day from homes in Seattle, Tacoma, Olympia, and other Puget Sound towns.

The wildflower meadows of Paradise and the higher, drier, east-side destination of Sunrise—closed by snow in winter—are the main focus for visitors to Mount Rainier in summer. Fewer visitors stop at the unique old-growth forest known as Grove of the Patriarchs on an island in the Ohanapecosh River on the southeast side of the park or the only temperate rainforest outside the Olympic Peninsula at Carbon River on the northwest side. And only a small but persistent trickle of hardy hikers attempt the 90-mile round-the-park Wonderland Trail, which links all these areas.

By late morning buses and cars circle the large parking lot at Paradise, and parking spaces have become like gold dust. Crowds wander between Jackson Visitor Center and the enormous historic Paradise Inn, whose timbered lobby is filled with people waiting to eat lunch in the dining room. Small family groups drift slowly along the network of developed paths winding toward the high country. Some head over the ridge for views of Nisqually Glacier. Others meander to waterfalls, hike to mirror-smooth lakes, or venture higher on the Skyline Trail above Panorama Point, gateway to the upper mountain.

The air at this 5,400-foot elevation is warm, but above, the 14,410-foot mountain summit is haloed in one of its familiar UFO-shaped lenticular clouds. The Mountain, as it is referred to locally, is so high it makes its own weather, bringing rain, snow, and perpetual high, cold winds to its summit. Even in midsummer, it is a broad-shouldered, snowy hulk, an Arctic island surrounded by green temperate forests and fractious rivers. It has 25 permanent glaciers—the largest number for any single peak in the Lower 48.

Paradise held the record for the most snow accumulation in Washington, but the winter of 2004–2005 sounded warning bells for climate change, with just 400 inches measured by May 15—70 percent of the average accumulation. As a result, Rainier's glaciers have shrunk noticeably. But their sheer number make Mount Rainier the most potentially dangerous active volcano in the Cascades. Sulferous steam in the twin summit craters is perpetually present. The Mountain would barely have to clear its throat to cause a catastrophic Mount St. Helen's type avalanche mudflow, or lahar. It's happened at least 60 times since the Ice Age ended, and will certainly happen again.

By far the largest lahar was the Osceola Mudflow, 5,600 years ago, which collapsed 2,000 feet of the old mountaintop and tore through the White River Valley to expand the Puget Sound shoreline. Communities like Puyallup are built on ancient Rainier mudflows. Even more frequent are smaller glacial outburst flows, filled with glacial ice blocks and boulders, which reshape the valleys. Fifteen of these glacial outburst flows have raced down river valleys since 1986 alone.

All this weighed heavily on my mind as I lay in my tent at Cougar Rock Campground, listening to the low, constant roar of glacial icemelt tumbling over house-sized boulders in the Nisqually River. In Tahoma's shadow, I can feel its pent-up energy.

Alpine tarn and clearing evening fog. PHOTO ©ALAN MAJCHROWICZ

Christine Falls, Van Trump Creek, and highway bridge. PHOTO ©TERRY DONNELLY

Western redcedar trunks in Grove of The Patriarchs. PHOTO ©CHARLES GURCHE

It is palpable in a way that never registered with me when, as a Seattle resident, I would watch Mount Rainier emerge from weeks of cloud and excitedly call my friends, saying "The Mountain's out." In fact, you can only take in Mount Rainier from a distance. From close range, it seems to shrink from view and lodge in your imagination, growing larger and more terrifying as your other senses take over.

A small group of climbers pass me, enroute to Camp Muir. They are taking their time getting to the overnight camp, where they will rise at 1 a.m. to make their assault on the summit. More than 10,000 people attempt the climb every year, most guided by the Rainier Mountaineering, Inc., operated by the famed mountaineer. Lou Whittacker. Only half those who attempt the summit make it. For sea-level residents, elevation is a major factor. You need to spend time getting used to being in the thinner alpine air. One night at 10,400-foot Camp Muir may not be enough.

John Muir, for whom Camp Muir was named, was accustomed to spending days in the Sierra Nevada mountains with just a handful of tea and a crust of bread, but he was an exceptional case. He climbed Mount Rainier in 1888 with artist William Keith, Seattle photographer Arthur Warner, E. S. Ingraham, and Philemon B. Van Trump. The articles Muir wrote over the years helped get the park set aside in 1899. It was just in time. Rainier's lowland forests were fast being clearcut and mining claims were rapidly growing. The subalpine meadows were already being grazed by sheep, and trampled to death by visitors. Despite the paths, overuse of fragile meadows remains a pressing problem today.

Muir's ascent was by no means the first. Bushwacking through dense surrounding forests in 1870, Van Trump and his companion Hazard Stevens, son of first Washington governor Isaac Stevens, were the first to make a recorded ascent of the peak, guided by a Yakama Indian named Chief Sluiskin. Sluiskin, whose people witnessed the 1820 and 1854 eruptions of Mount Rainier, did his best to dissuade the men from venturing above the snowfields. But Stevens believed it could be done. Lieutenant August Kautz had proven that in 1857, when bad weather had forced him to turn back near the summit.

On their return, Van Trump and Stevens helped found an alpine climbing group that would eventually become The Mountaineers, an organization that has rallied support for all of Washington's national parks and wilderness areas over more than a century. Van Trump guided a growing number of Puget Sound region settlers to the top of Mount Rainier, and people saw for themselves the beauty of The Mountain.

Among them was James Longmire, who himself would take up guiding from the hot springs resort he built in the forest below. Today, Longmire National Historic District highlights rustic architecture and the human history of the park, with an historic inn, a store, park administrative building, Longmire Museum, and a Transportation Museum in a tiny, disused gas station. Unlike Paradise, which is buried by snow in winter, Longmire is open year round. The 1.2-mile walking tour around the district and gentle trails through the forest are the perfect introduction to Mount Rainier, which, on clear days, can be seen beckoning the faithful ever nearer to Paradise.

Unicorn Peak and Foss Peak in the Tatoosh Range, winter evening. PHOTO ©PAT O'HARA

MOUNT RAINIER

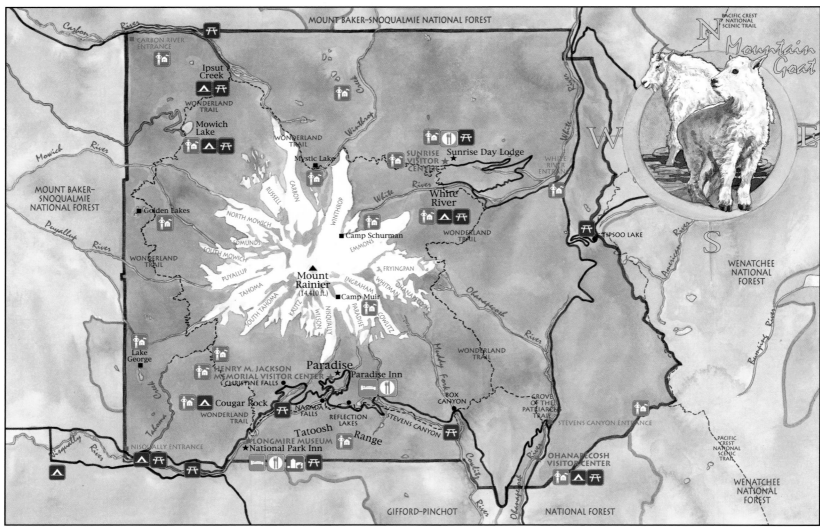

MOUNT BAKER–SNOQUALMIE NATIONAL FOREST

Carbon River
CARBON RIVER ENTRANCE
Ipsut Creek
WONDERLAND TRAIL
Mowich Lake
WONDERLAND TRAIL
Mystic Lake
SUNRISE VISITOR CENTER
Sunrise Day Lodge
WHITE RIVER ENTRANCE
MOUNT BAKER–SNOQUALMIE NATIONAL FOREST
Mowich River
Golden Lakes
NORTH MOWICH
RUSSELL
CARBON
WINTHROP
White River
WONDERLAND TRAIL
Puyallup River
SOUTH MOWICH
EDMUNDS
Camp Schurman
EMMONS
TIPSOO LAKE
WONDERLAND TRAIL
PUYALLUP
Mount Rainier (14,410 ft.)
FRYINGPAN
WENATCHEE NATIONAL FOREST
Lake George
TAHOMA
SOUTH TAHOMA
KAUTZ
WILSON
NISQUALLY
Camp Muir
PARADISE
WHITMAN
OHANAPECOSH
HENRY M. JACKSON MEMORIAL VISITOR CENTER
CHRISTINE FALLS
Paradise
Paradise Inn
WONDERLAND TRAIL
Cougar Rock
NARADA FALLS
REFLECTION LAKES
BOX CANYON
STEVENS CANYON
GROVE OF THE PATRIARCHS TRAIL
STEVENS CANYON ENTRANCE
PACIFIC CREST NATIONAL SCENIC TRAIL
Tatoosh Range
LONGMIRE MUSEUM
National Park Inn
NISQUALLY ENTRANCE
Nisqually River
OHANAPECOSH VISITOR CENTER
WENATCHEE NATIONAL FOREST
GIFFORD–PINCHOT NATIONAL FOREST

Mountain Goat

ILLUSTRATION BY DARLECE CLEVELAND

SIZE: 235,625 acres. **FOUNDED:** 1899. 97 percent of park designated as wilderness in 1988. National Historic Landmark District in 1997. **HIGHLIGHTS:** Washington's tallest volcano and fifth highest peak in the contiguous U.S., 14,410-foot Mount Rainier, covered in 36 square miles of snow and ice. National record for snow: 1122 inches of annual snowfall at Paradise Meadow. Nisqually is mountain's most accessible glacier; Emmons, its largest and highest accessible glacier; Carbon, its longest, thickest, and lowest-elevation glacier. Hiking, camping, and picknicking in old-growth lowland forests, including giant trees in Grove of the Patriarchs near Ohanapecosh and temperate rainforest in Carbon River Valley. Subalpine wildflower meadows at Paradise and Sunrise. National historic landmark district at Longmire. Historic lodges at Longmire and Paradise. Scenic driving and high-elevation climbing. **SEEING THE PARK:** Nisqually Entrance, SR 706 via SR 7 from Tacoma, leads to popular Longmire and Paradise areas from Interstate 5. White River Entrance, via SR 410 on northeast side, leads to Sunrise Visitor Center, wildflower meadows, and views of Emmons Glacier. SR 410 (Stephen Mather Memorial Parkway) leads south to Stevens Canyon Entrance via SR 123 and Ohanapecosh area. Carbon River Entrance deadends at Ipsut Creek in the northwest corner; nearby Mowich Lake has its own entrance on SR 165. **VISITOR and INFORMATION CENTERS AND MUSEUMS:** Longmire Museum (tel. 360-569-2211 ext. 3314); Jackson Visitor Center, Paradise (tel. 360-569-2211 x 2328); Ohanapecosh Visitor Center (tel. 360-569-6046); Sunrise Visitor Center (tel 360-663-2425); Longmire Wilderness Information Center (tel. 360-569-HIKE); Climbing Information Center at the Paradise Guide House (tel. 360-569-6009); White River WIC (tel. 360-569-6030); Carbon River Ranger Station, northside camping and climbing permits (tel. 360-829-5127. **HIKING:** 90-mile Wonderland Trail links the whole park and can be hiked in segments. Demanding and requires advance planning. Easy hikes include 0.7-mile Trail of the Shadows at Longmire; 1-mile Myrtle Falls at Paradise; 0.5-mile Emmons Vista Trail at Sunrise; and 1.5-mile Grove of the Patriarchs at Ohanapecosh. **CAMPGROUNDS:** Sunshine Point (year round, 18 sites), Cougar Rock Campground (172 sites) near Longmire; White River Campground (112 sites) near Sunrise; Ohanapecosh Campground (188 sites). Ipsut Creek (year round, 22 sites); Mowich Lake (walk-in, 30 sites). **SPECIAL CONSIDERATIONS:** Advance reservations for Cougar Rock and Ohanapecosh Campgrounds recommended between Memorial Day and Labor Day. No gas in the park. Carbon River Road and Nisqually entrance to Paradise are open year round; the rest of the roads in the park close in winter. Climbing permits are required above 10,000 feet or on glaciers; all overnight trips into park backcountry require a permit. New climbers are strongly urged to use one of Rainier's mountain guide services. **PARK CONTACT INFORMATION:** Mount Rainier National Park, 55210 238th Avenue East, Ashford, WA 98304; 360-569-2211; www.nps.gov/mora.

NORTH CASCADES

Aerial view of the Picket Range, early winter. PHOTO ©TERRY DONNELLY

The North Cascades have the most distinctive appearance of any mountain range in the Northwest. Razor-sharp pinnacles, doffed caprocks, steep castellated ramparts, and the towering white hulk of dormant, but not extinct, Mount Baker parallel Interstate 5 between Everett and British Columbia, a forbidding yet intriguing sight. North Cascades National Park and Ross Lake and Lake Chelan National Recreation Areas have been managed as a single National Park Service complex since 1968, and are the core of a large protected area that also includes the Mount Baker, Pasayten, and Glacier Peak wilderness areas, national forest lands, and provincial parks in British Columbia.

The National Park Service Complex was set aside after a long bitter fight between environmentalists and natural resource extraction industries. Although historic communities line the low valleys, 93 percent of the park's 684,313 acres are managed as the Stephen Mather Wilderness. The intact ecosystem even includes grizzly bears, long extirpated elsewhere.

The North Cascades look different from the rest of the Cascades, and they are. Born as 400-million-year-old volcanic islands in the Pacific Ocean, they accreted to North America as the oceanic ridge spread outward, widening the ocean and creating what is now western Washington. Unlike the more youthful Cascades, they are not volcanic—although the 35-million-year-old volcanoes of Mount Baker and Glacier Peak lie nearby—but a mosaic of crumpled terranes that were forced up by seismic forces.

Some 312 glaciers—more than found in any national park in the Lower 48—are found in the National Park Service Complex. They ebb and flow with the seasons, compressing into ice crystals from the deep snowpack in winter then melting and shrinking as temperatures warm up in summer. Here it feels as if the Ice Age never ended, especially in winter, when the precipitous peaks of Mount Shuksan and other summits rise out of the gray winter storms above Concrete, Marblemount, and Darrington, their pristine facades in complete contrast to the gritty little logging towns.

The weight of the glaciers crushes everything in sight, and as gravity forces them to flow downward, they carve wide U-shaped valleys filled with ground-up gravel bars and frigid river water cloudy with rock flour. A glacier's calling card is knifelike arete ridges, scooped-out cirque basins, huge stranded erratic boulders, striated and polished river valley walls, and deep moraines that plug lakes and create ever-changing riverbeds.

This highland drama ends very differently in the low country of the Skagit River Valley, as the river slows and reaches Puget Sound. In summer, La Conner is postcard-pretty next to tulip fields and adjoining Fidalgo Island, home to the Swinomish Tribe, one of eight different contemporary Native American and Canadian First Nation groups associated with the National Park Service complex. Ferries bound for the San Juan Islands leave from Anacortes. Day trippers meander along the North Cascades Highway (SR 20), the most popular scenic drive in Washington, stopping to enjoy homemade organic ice cream filled with fresh blueberries at famous Cascadian Farm, near Marblemount.

By fall, pumpkins have replaced tulips and berries, and salmon are returning up the Skagit River, as they have for thousands of years. In winter, one of the largest gatherings of bald eagles in the Lower 48 will descend on the river, to feast on the carcasses of the salmon near Rockport. In early October, vine maple are the color of red wine, as crisper days bring out "leaf peepers" in the thousands. It starts to freeze by the end of the month, chasing campers from the east side of the mountains, where hot summer days are replaced by winter nights with plummeting temperatures. Park visitor services mostly close down at Stehekin, the tiny isolated community at the head of Lake Chelan that has been a favorite getaway all summer. Typically, by mid-November, State Route 20 is closed by heavy winter snow at Milepost 134, just west of the Cascade Crest, and won't open again until April—depending on snow and avalanche conditions.

Park headquarters at Sedro-Woolley, a few miles east of Interstate 5, is a good stop for information and maps, but the best place to learn about the natural and cultural history of North Cascades is 55 miles on, at the main visitor center at Newhalem.

OPPOSITE: Mount Shuksan from Picture Lake, Mount Baker–Snoqualmie National Forest. **PAGE 28/29:** Glacial landscape of Boston Basin, sunset. PHOTO ©ALAN MAJCHROWICZ
PHOTO ©JOHN MARSHALL

The Triplets and Cascade Peak, near Cascade Pass. PHOTO ©JOHN BARGER

Diablo Lake and North Cascades Highway. PHOTO ©JOHN MARSHALL

Vine maples and mossy boulders along the Skagit River. PHOTO ©D.A. HORCHNER

The visitor center, open year round, is a beautiful soaring wood-and-glass structure in the cool, coniferous forests bordering the Skagit. Here, you can talk to a ranger about your trip, buy books, watch a theater presentation, view interesting museum exhibits, walk on short accessible interpretive trails into the woods, and camp in two pleasant

campgrounds.

Newhalem is a company town constructed by Seattle City Light beginning in 1918, when the dam on the Skagit started producing hydroelectric power for nearby Seattle. Seattle City Light cruises on Diablo Lake have been popular with Seattle residents for generations. Newhalem is now much less populated. You can park and walk around. A walking tour brochure available at the information center describes the town's history and offers information on several easy hikes in the gorge, including one that takes you up to beautiful gardens planted by the company.

The area has always been a popular fishing and hunting area for Upper Skagit Indians. Remains of a 600-year-old canoe launch were found near Goodell Creek Campground, and a trail from Newhalem leads to a 1,400-year-old Indian rock shelter. The name Newhalem is a corruption of a Lushootseed word meaning "place where the goats are snared" and, in winter, the high cliffs above the gorge are a great spot to see shaggy-coated mountain goats.

A very small percentage of North Cascades National Park Service Complex's 450,000 annual visitors come to hike, which means that you may have the high country to yourself. Trails are very steep and challenging and leave from SR 20 along its length. Thunder Creek Trail departs from the south side of SR 20, at Colonial Creek Campground on Diablo Lake, the manmade reservoir created by Diablo Dam, while the trail to Sourdough Mountain heads from the north side. Trails to Ross Lake, the long skinny manmade reservoir that can be boated all the way to Hozomeen, just south of the U.S.-Canada boundary, are nearby. Among the most accessible of east-side trails is 1-mile Rainy Lake Trail, which leads to a waterfall and glacier views. You can continue to Maple Pass from here. At 5,477 feet, Washington Pass is the highest point on the highway. The road continues into the Methow Valley via Winthrop.

If I had to choose only one trail that captures the history and beauty of the North Cascades, I'd probably opt for the 7.4-mile round trip Cascade Pass Trail. Stop at the Wilderness Information Center in Marblemount for road and trail updates, then travel the 23.1-mile Cascade River Road to the trailhead opposite Johannesburg Mountain. The gravel road follows the river all the way, passing two riverside national forest campgrounds; the road is quite narrow and steep in places, so is not recommended for RVs. In the parking lot at the trailhead, the sight and sound of glacial ice falling from hanging valleys created by Johannesburg Glacier are alone worth the drive.

Bring plenty of water: it can feel like steep going in summer on the 3 miles of switchbacks through the woods. Apply strong insect repellent to deter persistent biting black flies if you hike in midsummer. The bugs disappear as you get to cooler, windier elevations on top. Seasoned hikers like to continue into adjoining glacial valleys and ridges, including Sahale Arm and the Stehekin River Valley, at the head of glacial Lake Chelan. Cascade Pass was an important Indian route through the North Cascades and was used in 1811 by Alexander Ross, a fur trader with John Jacob Astor; later, gold and silver miners passed this way. You probably won't see a grizzly, but you might glimpse a hoary marmot, black bear, or mountain goat in subalpine meadows filled with a changing display of wildflowers and mountain heather.

Sunset seen from above Lake Chelan. PHOTO ©JOHN MARSHALL

NORTH CASCADES

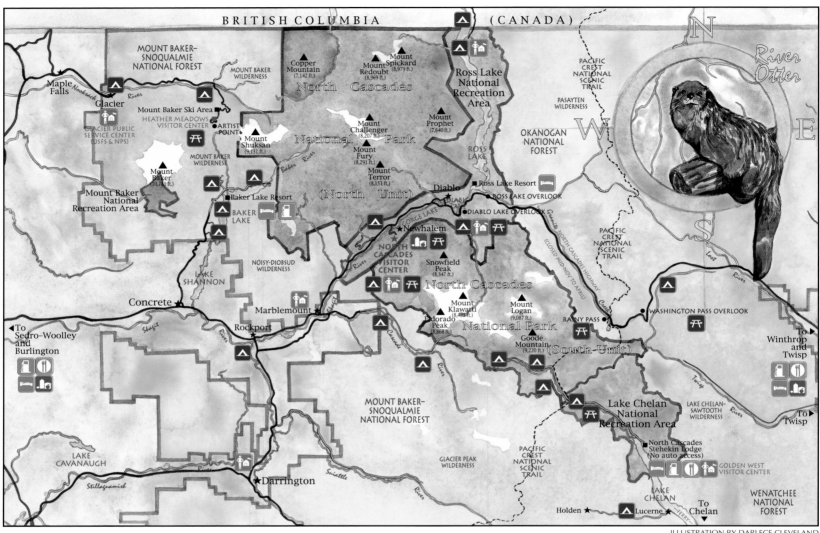

ILLUSTRATION BY DARLECE CLEVELAND

SIZE: 684,313 acres. **FOUNDED:** 1968; 93 percent of the park designated Stephen Mather Wilderness in 1988. **LOCATION:** Northwest Washington in the North Cascades, east of Mount Vernon and Bellingham. North Cascades Highway (SR 20) crosses the North Cascades to Methow Valley. You can make a North Cascades Loop by continuing on SR 153 through Winthrop, Twisp, and Wenatchee, then back to Interstate 5 on SR 2, paralleling the Skykomish River Valley, via Leavenworth. Bordered by the Mount Baker-Snoqualmie, Wenatchee, and Okanogan National Forests, including seven wilderness areas, and three provincial parks in British Columbia. **HIGHLIGHTS:** Recently glaciated mountain range with more glaciers than any other park in the Lower 48 and many glacial features. The park's 9,000 feet of vertical relief and the great contrast between climates east and west of the Cascade crest provide habitat for one of the greatest diversities of plant life in North America and for varied animals including rare, sensitive, and endangered species such as grizzly bears. Many lakes, including Ross Lake and Lake Chelan. Three historic hydroelec-

tric power plants and dams on the Skagit River provide 25 percent of Seattle's electricity. Historic logging and mining settlements at Sedro-Woolley, Darrington, Marblemount, and Concrete; ranching and farming in Winthrop, Twisp, Wenatchee; mountain resort at Leavenworth. Puget Sound communities at Anacortes, La Conner, Mount Vernon, Bellingham, and Everett. Farms, state parks, eagle watching sites, and salmon runs along the Wild and Scenic Skagit River. Three historic districts in park, and over 250 archaeological sites. Eight contemporary Indian tribes, including the Swinomish, Sauk-Suiattle, and Upper Skagit tribes. **SEEING THE PARK:** SR 20 has many scenic viewpoints, hiking trails, campgrounds, and communities along the way. Summer is peak time for travel on lakes. Late summer is peak time for berries and salmon. Fall foliage is peak time for scenic driving. Winter viewing of bald eagles along the Skagit. **VISITOR CENTERS:** Sedro-Woolley: National Park Headquarters and Mount Baker Ranger District (tel. 360-856-5700, ext. 515, open year round; Newhalem: North Cascades Visitor Center (tel. 206-386-4495, open daily year round; weekends

only, from mid-November to mid-April); Marblemount: Wilderness Information Center, (summer only: tel. 360-873-4500 ext. 39); Stehekin: Golden West Visitor Center (tel. 360-856-5700 ext. 340, then 14, seasonal only); Okanogan National Forest: North Cascades Scenic Highway Visitor Center—Winthrop, Methow Valley, (tel. 509-996-4000); Wenatchee National Forest: Lake Chelan Ranger District (tel. 509-682-2576 USFS and 2549 NPS). **LODGES:** North Cascades Stehekin Lodge, Lake Chelan, and Ross Lake Resort, Ross Lake, open seasonally. **CAMPGROUNDS:** SR 20, Mileposts 81-180: Rasar and Rockport State Parks; Howard Miller Steelhead Park; Goodell, Newhalem, and Colonial Creeks; Lone Fir, Klipchuck, and Early Winters. Cascade River Road: Marble Creek and Mineral Park. **SPECIAL CONSIDERATIONS:** State Route 20 closes mid-Nov–April, depending on snow and avalanche conditions. Boat schedule and hiking at Stehekin is tricky: plan on staying at least one night at Stehekin, if you want to hike.

Greywolf Ridge seen from Blue Mountain area. PHOTO ©PAT O'HARA

OLYMPIC

Slugs are one of the big draws in the Hoh Rain Forest, the rainiest place in the Lower 48. The gift shop at a cafe outside Olympic National Park, is awash in slug paraphernalia, from slug-shaped carvings to mugs, T-shirts, and bumper stickers; the owners have even been known to tether a giant slug outside on the lush green grass to attract visitors.

Today, though, is definitely not optimum slug weather. We're deep in the drought days of August, the temperature is 80 degrees, and it hasn't rained for over a week. A clear blue sky spreads itself out above the steep Hoh River Valley—one of a number of river valleys carved by glaciers in the 6,000 – 8,000-foot-elevation Olympic Mountains.

Even at sea level, the signs of the glaciation that carved the Olympic Peninsula during the last ice age are everywhere: rocky gray glacial till, known as moraine, dumped by gravity into deep banks and bars that shuss loudly as water pours over and round them; rock flour, the ground-up residue of more than 60 glaciers in the Olympics, clouding the icy rivers as they race to the sea; and deep, clear bodies of water like Lake Crescent, an Ice Age relic, like so much else on the peninsula, with its own unique species of trout found nowhere else.

It's hard to get used to the rainforest in summer. Instead of leaf drip and muffled gloom, the thick canopy is penetrated by an incandescent lemon-lime glow, just as morning sun streaming through a clerestory window in a cathedral illuminates an altar. Shafts of light fall on leaf litter in a clearing, spotlighting insects, butterflies, and the occasional Roosevelt elk footprint in the mud. The sun's rays dance around the scalloped edges of big-leafed maples and down-pointed fingertips of western hemlock in an ever-changing series of fractals, like colored prisms in a child's kaleidoscope.

Mosses and ferns, luxuriant in the rainy season, are hunkered down for the summer. Hikers take along water bottles on trails now instead of breathing in wet vapor to stay hydrated. Slugs, which thrive in the 100 percent humidity, are holed up in damp nooks, along with salamanders and other amphibians. The sounds of children frolicking in the frigid river and the red-jacketed flashes of passing kayakers only adds to the sense of disorientation.

During the four years I lived in Seattle, I came to Olympic frequently to escape writing deadlines, noisy neighbors, and urban living. Jumping aboard one of the frequent ferries on the Seattle waterfront, in minutes I would have the wind in my hair, the spray in my face, and be off on a quick, inexpensive adventure to a place once considered so foreboding, people thought that monsters lived there. Even today, there are no roads through the Olympics: the only way around the peninsula is to drive Highway 101, the road that encircles it, or backpack across the mountains.

I love to walk on Rialto Beach and explore tidepools exposed by the low tide at Hole in the Wall, then sit sheltered in the 50-foot-long peeled tree trunks deposited onto the beach by winter storms. On this 73-mile wild Pacific Ocean coastline, the longest in the country, I have drawn mandalas charting my life in the wet sand, talked about salmon and logging with Quileute fishermen at La Push, marveled over ancient artifacts at the Makah cultural museum in Neah Bay, and spotted gray whales in winter at Kalaloch. Among the colonnaded forests of towering Sitka spruce and western hemlock, I've set up camp and spent whole days reading, as rain and fog swirled around me, feeling safe, cocooned, and serene.

Landscape and culture are inextricably linked on the Olympic Peninsula. On one trip, I was driving along Highway 101 when I was startled by the sudden appearance of a bald eagle near Dungeness Spit. Swooping low over my car, the raptor fixed me with a beady, intelligent stare I knew well from ravens in the desert Southwest. I realized then that I had been daydreaming, driving too fast to catch my ferry home, and was missing what I always cherished so much about the Olympic Peninsula: its spectacular wildlife. I decided to take a few minutes to visit the Jamestown S'Kllalam Tribe's Native Art gallery at Sequim Bay, something I had never allowed myself time to do before. As I browsed the classic northwestern Indian art, I struck up a conversation with a delightful woman, a tribal elder who had recently returned to her village

Pink heather and Mount Olympus from High Divide. PHOTO ©PAT O'HARA

Big-leaf maple on the shore of Crescent Lake. PHOTO ©LARRY ULRICH

Driftwood on the rocky shore of Ruby Beach. PHOTO ©TERRY DONNELLY

after years away. I asked her which piece I should buy and the woman handed me a traditional bentwood box of red cedar painted with a stylized eagle. "Take this," she said, unaware of my earlier encounter. "It will give you strength."

Native people see animals as teachers, and so do I. On another occasion, I was drawn to a pair of Native-made pewter earrings showing Raven, the creator and trickster hero of Northwest tribes, carrying a seed of wisdom in his beak. After 20 years of vegetarianism, I found myself often needing to eat salmon, a spiritual food for thousands of years in the Northwest. One fall, while descending 5,757-foot Hurricane Hill, I followed in the footsteps of black bears as I dropped 5,300 feet into the Elwha River Valley, one of the park's loveliest rivers. Animal life is a palpable presence everywhere here—wilderness never far away from human settlements.

In 1992, Olympic National Park finally received President H. W. Bush's signature on an agreement to purchase and decommission two dams on the river. Over the last century, the dams—now no longer needed by the Port Angeles paper mills they served—have destroyed the record-breaking runs of pink and other salmon that once returned to spawn annually in the headwaters, a living link between the mountains and the ocean that nourished the whole ecosystem.

After the dams are removed—scheduled to begin in 2009—salmon and steelhead will again be able to spawn annually in the Elwha watershed. After 30 years of restoration, it's estimated that as many as 392,000 smolts will be produced in the river by returning fish. These are dark times for wild Northwest salmon, which are in steep decline everywhere due to overfishing, dams, logging, hatchery degradation, and pollution. Every year, Northwest tribes honor the first returning salmon with a Homecoming ceremony. In their stories, salmon are people who live below the ocean and must be appeased with offerings. There hasn't been much to celebrate recently, but now there's hope.

Brits like myself were among the first to explore the Olympic Peninsula. In March 1778, Captain Cook named Cape Flattery because an opening in the coast "flattered" the captain and crew with the hope of finding harbor. In 1787, another British captain named Charles William Barkley recognized the passage between the Olympic Peninsula and Vancouver Island and entered it on his charts as the Strait of Juan de Fuca, for the Greek navigator sailing for Spain who had claimed it in 1592. On July 4, 1788, British captain John Meares named Mount Olympus and explored the strait. And in 1792, Captain George Vancouver named the geographical features of the region, including Dungeness, Discovery Bay, the Olympic Mountains, Hood Canal, Mount Rainier, and Vancouver Island.

Nationality, however, has nothing to do with what brings me back to the Olympic Peninsula again and again. For this unique ecosystem has its own nationality and culture, and speaks to me through its inhabitants in a language all its own. Slugs, of course, are part of the story. Like the 23 endemic species that only make their home on the Olympic Peninsula after the Ice Age isolated them, slugs have adapted magnificently and now boast more species on the peninsula than anywhere else in the Northwest. Just don't tell newcomers it sometimes doesn't rain in the rainforest. They won't believe you.

Sol Duc Falls on the Sol Duc River. PHOTO ©PAT O'HARA

OLYMPIC NATIONAL PARK

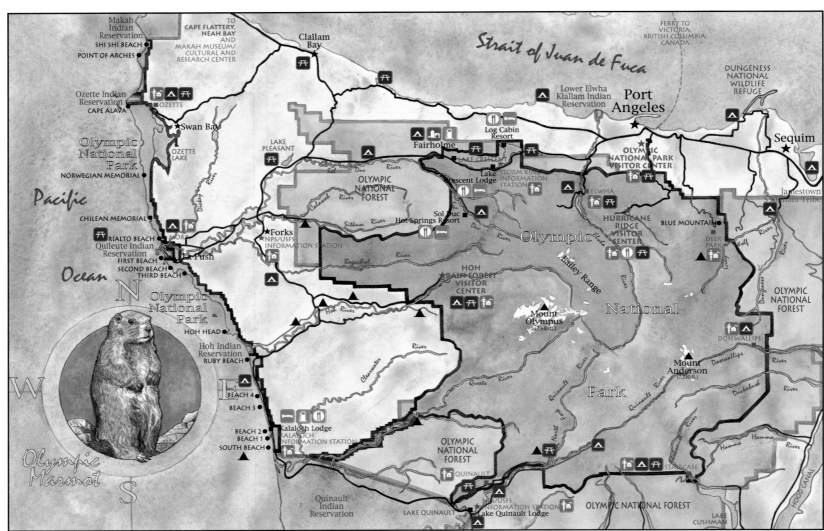

ILLUSTRATION BY DARLECE CLEVELAND

SIZE: 1,442 square miles of the 6,400-square-mile Olympic Peninsula is contained in the national park. **FOUNDED:** 1,500,000 acres of old-growth forests protected as Olympic Forest Reserve in 1897; 615,000-acre Mount Olympus National Monument designated in 1909 to protect Roosevelt elk in upper rainforest valleys. National park designation came on June 29, 1938; a UNESCO World Biosphere Reserve in 1976; a World Heritage Site in 1981; and 95 percent (876,699 acres) set aside as wilderness on November 16, 1988. **LOCATION:** Northwest Washington, on the Olympic Peninsula, bordered by the Pacific Ocean. Scenic drives leave from US Highway 101, which encircles the peninsula. **ELEVATIONS:** Sea level to 7,980 feet at Mount Olympus. **HIGHLIGHTS:** A superb temperate old-growth rain forest grows on the west side of the peninsula, reaching 200 feet tall and 30 feet thick on the 120-167 inches of annual rainfall; 73 miles of wild Pacific Ocean coastline, including tide pools at Hole in the Wall and Indian petroglyphs and 144 million-year-old rocks at Point of Arches; Hurricane Ridge in the

6,000- to 8,000-foot elevation Olympic Mountains; 266 glaciers and 13 glacial river valleys; 10 unique runs of coho, Chinook, sockeye, pink, chum, and steelhead salmon on the Elwha River; Lakes Crescent and Quinault; Lake Ozette; Olympic Coast National Marine Sanctuary borders the park; Dungeness National Wildlife Refuge is located near the park on the Strait of Juan de Fuca; Sol Duc Hot Springs; 8 Indian tribes have traditional ties to the park: the Makah; Hoh; Quileute; Quinault; Skokomish; Squaxin; Jamestown S'Kllalam; Lower Elwha Klallam. **SEEING THE PARK:** Car ferries from Seattle cross to Bainbridge Island. Agate Bridge links Bainbridge Island with Kitsap Peninsula, and Hood Canal Bridge connects the Kitsap and Olympic Peninsulas. On the Olympic Peninsula, US Highway 101 leads to all the main sights. **VISITOR CENTERS and SCENIC DRIVES:** Main scenic drive, park headquarters, visitor center, and wilderness center in Port Angeles; scenic drive and visitor center at Hoh Rain Forest, southeast of Forks; Ranger stations at Mora, Kalaloch, Lakes Crescent and Ozette, Sol

Duc, Elwha, Eagle, Deer Park, and Quinault Rain Forest; Staircase and Dosewallips River; backcountry ranger stations at Enchanted Valley, Olympus, Elkhorn, and Low Divide are intermittently staffed seasonally. **CAMPGROUNDS:** Heart o' the Hills, Graves, Elwha, North Fork, Ozette, Queets, South Beach, Sol Duc, Deer Park, Dosewallips, Staircase, Mora, Kalaloch, Fairholme, Altair, and Hoh, and many designated backcountry sites; additional campsites in Olympic National Forest. **PARK CONTACT INFORMATION:** Olympic National Park, 600 East Park Avenue, Port Angeles, WA 98362; tel. (360) 565-3130; www.nps.gov/olym.

OPPOSITE: Massive driftwood at Rialto Beach. PHOTO ©PAT O'HARA

View from Johnston Ridge, sunrise, July 1998. PHOTO ©JEFFREY L. TORRETTA

Mount St. Helens

"Vancouver, Vancouver, this is it!" The excited recorded voice of David Johnston, the US Geological Survey geologist who perished in the May 18, 1980, eruption at Mount St. Helens, eerily fills the auditorium of the volcano observatory named in his honor, as the multi-media presentation simulating the events of that day fills the movie screen.

There are other excellent movies about the latest eruption of 40,000-year-old Mount St. Helens, the youngest of the Cascade volcanoes. The Mount St. Helens Visitor Center at Silver Lake, operated by Washington State Department of Parks and Recreation, is dedicated to the human story of the monument and examines the implications for the thousands of Puget Sound residents living directly in the path of Washington's dangerous volcanic eruptions and mudflows. And the large-screen Cinedome Theater at Castle Rock offers exciting live footage of the eruption.

But nothing has prepared me for the emotional power of this state-of-the-art, blow-by-blow reenactment of the volcano's eruption. Cleverly conceived from start to finish, the presentation ends with a masterful touch that takes full advantage of the unique setting. The audience remains seated, the movie screen disappears, the curtains part, and the front of the theater is revealed to be huge picture windows with the real Mount St. Helens looming like a gape-mouthed behemoth just five miles away. Now, that's entertainment!

Putting yourself—if only virtually—in the path of the dangerous eruption that killed Johnston, who by sheer bad luck was the one monitoring earthquake activity near here that quiet Sunday morning—is both sobering and educational. It's just one of many extraordinary visitor experiences at 110,000-acre Mount St. Helens National Volcanic Monument. Ghostly gray lifecasts of real people form tableaux at the human history museum. A nature talk is conducted by an amazingly lifelike holographic ranger at Coldwater Ridge Visitor Center. And at Johnston Ridge Volcano Observatory, you can learn factoids via touch-screen computers, watch a live seismometer recording earthquakes happening on the mountain in real time, and jump on a platform to create your own earthquake.

Unlike most monuments, which are managed by the National Park Service, Mount St. Helens is managed by the US Forest Service. The monument was established in 1982 to protect the fragile volcanic features and allow scientists and the public the unique opportunity to watch a landscape recover following a volcanic eruption. I've never met such enthusiastic and knowledgeable young rangers, all of them passionate about the work they do and ready to engage young and old. Perhaps it's the energy of the volcano, which simmers in the background as they welcome visitors who drive Spirit Lake Highway 504 to pay homage to the mountain. Whatever it is, it's contagious.

The 1980 eruption was hardly a surprise, after swarms of earthquakes had begun in March, 1980, but the form it would take was unknown, and the state nervously watched and waited. On May 18, a 5.1 Richter-scale earthquake at 8:32 a.m. triggered a massive landslide averaging 150 feet deep, and as much as 620 feet deep at the base of the mountain. In seconds, huge slabs of rock and ice slammed into Spirit Lake and surged over part of Johnston Ridge, but the bulk of the landslide roared 14 miles down the Toutle River Valley. The pressurized gases inside what was once a perfect snowcapped volcano now freed themselves in a powerful 225–730 mph lateral blast. It instantly blew down 230 square miles of some of the loveliest old-growth forests in the Northwest, leaving behind splintered stumps, tree trunks strewn like matchsticks, and ghostly standing dead trees scorched by the intense heat. After the dust cleared, Mount St. Helens was unrecognizable. A huge crater, largely created when the north side and summit collapsed in the gigantic landslide, replaced the former 9,677-foot summit of the volcano.

The volcano, though, had only just begun to flex its muscles. A spectacular vertical column of ash and pumice, 15 miles high, erupted from the volcano, showering eastern Washington with grit that ruined car engines and blocked out the sun. The volcano continued to erupt for nine hours, but five smaller volcanic eruptions also occurred that summer, and different areas

Douglas fir and lupine at Lahar, south side of mountain. PHOTO ©JACK DYKINGA

Devastation seen from Smith Creek Overlook. PHOTO ©PAT O'HARA

received ashfall depending on wind direction, including Puget Sound.

Nonexplosive eruptions continued for another six years, building the new dome to a height of 920 feet and 3,450 feet in length. In 2004, the volcano erupted again, closing all climbing routes to the volcano rim. The new dome in Mount St. Helens continues to grow, with lava coming to the surface at a rate that would fill a dump truck every fifteen seconds. At the present rate of growth, it's estimated that Mount St. Helens could fill in its crater and regain its former height in as little as one hundred years, a clear indication of how fast the landscape at the mountain is changing.

Most destructive of all on May 18, 1980, were the lahars, or mudflows, that raced down the sides of the volcano. These rivers of wet, concretelike mud and rock were fueled by the melting of glacial ice or from groundwater that oozed out of the landslide deposit. The largest mudflow roared down the North Fork of the Toutle River, choking everything in its trajectory—fish, wildlife, bridges, vehicles, and homes—on a well-worn centuries-old path to the Columbia River.

Miraculously, because it was Sunday and authorities had issued mandatory evacuations, only 57 people died, and nearly 200 survived. But it was an unmitigated disaster for wildlife. Scientists estimate that 1,500 elk, 5,000 black-tailed deer, 200 black bears, 11,000 hares, 15 mountain lions, 300 bobcats, 27,000 grouse, and 1,400 coyotes died that day. Heavy ashfall caused the deaths of many more, including large numbers of birds and insects, and damaged 26 lakes, killing some 11 million fish.

Because spring hadn't arrived at this high elevation, a surprising number of plants and animals survived the eruption sheltered from the fierce heat beneath snow, underground, or underwater. The timing of the eruption enabled a wide variety of insects, amphibians, small mammals, and small trees and plants to survive in these sheltered locations. Although the volcano's extreme changes to the landscape doomed some surviving plants and animals, others thrived. The legacy of these survivors can be clearly seen today on many hillsides in the blast zone that were covered with a protective blanket of snow on May 18, 1980.

Within weeks, plants such as fireweed, blackberry vines, lupines, pearly everlasting, and the first tiny tree seedlings were appearing, blown in on the breeze, along with insects. Some of the first large mammals to return were elk. Today, they wander the pumice plain below the volcano and can be seen from trails leading from the visitor centers and pullouts along the highway.

Federal, state, and county money have also been put into creating new businesses to help local residents in the path of the volcano who lost their livelihoods. Helicopter rides into the monument above the Toutle River Valley are popular from county-owned Hoffstadt Bluffs Visitor Center at Milepost 27. The Forest Learning Center, operated by Weyerhauser and Rocky Mountain Elk Foundation, at Milepost 33, offers a look at salvage logging and the creation of new tree farms outside the monument. The fast-growing monocultural plantations are a striking contrast to the natural processes at work inside the monument, where mixed old-growth forest will take hundreds of years to grow back.

The south and east sides of the monument through Gifford Pinchot National Forest also have contrasting vistas. Forest Service Road 25, the main eastside road, travels south from Randle to Swift Reservoir. At Iron Creek, narrow Forest Service Road 26 drops into the monument via the Norway and Independence Passes for views of Spirit Lake today from Windy Ridge Viewpoint and access to the Mount Margaret Backcountry. From Swift Reservoir, Forest Service Road 90 goes west to Cougar, where there are full services (it can also be reached via Highway 503 from Interstate 5). Among the attractions near here are Ape Cave, a 2,000-year-old lava tube, and Lava Canyon and Lahar, which interprets ancient lava flows uncovered by slurry from the 1980 eruption. National Forest Passes are required at these sites.

Mount St. Helens seen from Coldwater Lake. PHOTO ©JEFF NICHOLAS

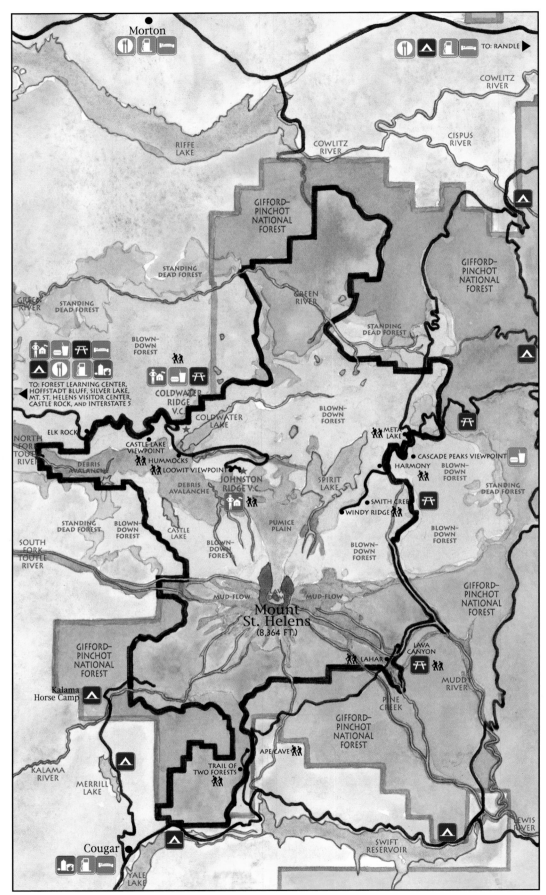

SIZE: 110,000 acres. **FOUNDED:** 1982. **LOCATION:** In the High Cascades of Southwest Washington, between Interstate 5 and Forest Route 25 and WA Highways 503 and 504. **ELEVATIONS:** 2,077 feet at Ape Cave to 4,314 feet at Johnston Ridge. **HIGHLIGHTS:** Vistas of a recently erupted active young Cascades volcano, volcanic rocks and formations, mountain lakes, forests, waterfalls, North Fork of Toutle River, and natural biological succession of returning plants and animals. **SEEING THE MONUMENT:** Stops along Spirit Lake Highway (Scenic Highway 504) from Castle Rock to Johnston Ridge include Mount St. Helen's National Volcanic Monument and wetlands at Silver Lake, first views of the altered course of the North Fork of Toutle River at Hoffstadt Bluffs Visitor Center, tree farm culture at Weyerhauser Forest Research Visitor Center, a new lake formed by the eruption at Castle Lake Viewpoint, Coldwater Ridge Visitor Center, Coldwater Lake Recreation Area, and Loowit Viewpoint, and closest views of the northside crater and volcano at Johnston Ridge Volcano Observatory. Short, easy interpretive trails from visitor centers include Eruption Trail from Johnston Ridge and Winds of Change from Coldwater Ridge. Forest Service Roads 99 and 26, on the northeast side of the volcano, have views of Spirit Lake at Windy Ridge Viewpoint. Hiking access at Norway and Independence Passes for Mount Margaret Backcountry and day hikes to Spirit Lake from Harmony Trail. Southwest section of the monument highlights include Lahar and Lava Canyon, Ape Cave, Trail of Two Forests, and Climber's Bivouac (permits required) off Highways 81 and 83. **VISITOR CENTERS:** Mount St. Helens Visitor Center (tel. 360-274-0962 for hours; open year round); Hoffstadt Bluffs Visitor Center; Weyerhauser Forest Research Center (daily, May to October only); Coldwater Ridge Visitor Center (tel. 360-274-2114 for hours and schedule); Johnston Ridge Volcano Observatory (tel. 360-274-2140 for hours; closed in winter). **CAMPGROUNDS:** Seaquest State Park, Highway 504, Silver Lake / Castle Rock, is across from the state-run visitor center. With 90 wooded sites and showers, it is most convenient for visiting the monument. USFS campgrounds on the east and south sides at Iron Creek (98 sites) and Lower Falls Recreation Area (42 sites) and Kalama (28 sites) and Lewis River (8 sites) Horse Camps; designated backcountry sites in Mount Margaret Backcountry. WA Department of Natural Resources campground at Merrill Lake (8 sites). Private PacifiCorp campgrounds with showers at Cresap Bay (73 sites), Cougar (60 sites), Beaver Bay (78 sites), and Swift Reservoir (93 sites). **SPECIAL CONSIDERATIONS:** Mount St. Helens continues to erupt! Check about trail and climbing closures. **MONUMENT CONTACT INFORMATION:** Mount St. Helens National Volcanic Monument, Gifford Pinchot National Forest, 42218 N.E. Yale Bridge Rd, Amboy, WA 98601; (360) 449-7800.

OPPOSITE: Mount Hood seen through blasted standing trees at Smith Creek Overlook. PHOTO ©LARRY ULRICH

COLUMBIA RIVER GORGE

The Columbia River, dawn from Rowena Crest Overlook. PHOTO ©JEFFREY L. TORRETTA

"Help! She's trying to kill us!" The young girl sitting next to the trail in Beacon Rock State Park is red in the face, her Harry Potter T-shirt dripping with sweat, but still able to joke as I pass by. Sprawled around her, legs outstretched and clearly pooped, is a small group of giggling 12-year-olds from a Portland summer camp program with their long-suffering counselor. She is dishing out water and snacks and congratulating her charges on having got half-way up the 1.25-mile trail to Hardy Falls, one of the most popular hikes on Columbia River Gorge National Scenic Area's Washington side. I find a tree stump far enough away to duck water fights and take a breather myself.

A break in the trees offers views to the sheer basaltic cliffs on the Oregon side, a mile across the legendary Columbia River. On this summer's day, cars and trains move swiftly side by side along Interstate 84 on the riverbank, racing at high speed through the 80-mile stretch of the Columbia River Gorge between Troutdale and The Dalles. Tugboats moving at a more sedate 5 mph as they push barges piled with French fries and wood chips head into Bonneville Dam and Lock, the first of the federal Columbia River dams to tame the river for flood control, irrigation, and hydro-electric power.

Above me is Hamilton Mountain; below me, Beacon Rock, the 850-foot-high core of an ancient volcano. It was named by William Clark, co-leader of the 1804-1806 cross-country Lewis and Clark Expedition, which camped here on November 2, 1805. It was near here on that day that the party first measured tidal influences on the Columbia River. They knew then that they were close to the Pacific Ocean, after 19 months of travel.

Beacon Rock had served as an important landmark on the river for millennia, both for the 80,000 Columbia River People who once lived and fished here and later for European settlers. In 1811, Alexander Ross of the John Jacob Astor expedition called the landmark "Inoshoack Castle," perhaps homesick for his native Scotland. To pioneers on the Oregon Trail who braved cascades on the Columbia River or bypassed the river and took the Barlow toll road around Mount Hood, it was Castle Rock.

After its name of Beacon Rock had been returned by the U.S. Board of Geographic Names, Henry J. Biddle bought it and constructed a one-mile trail to the top. His heirs sold it to the state in 1935, and the young men of Roosevelt's Civilian Conservation Corps worked their magic on the trails, campsites, and buildings of a new state park. The log structures they built are still in use today.

The 4,650-acre riverfront state park is one of a number of places to camp, hike, boat, fish, and learn about the history of Columbia River Gorge, the country's first national scenic area in 1986. Below the gentler, softly vegetated cliffs of the Washington side, you'll find a winding highway. From here, there are excellent views of the famous waterfalls pouring off the cooler, north-facing Oregon cliffs in the rainy season. Every community has services, including visitor centers and museums at Bonneville Dam and Lock, Skamania Lodge, Stevenson, Bingen, and Goldendale.

While the Washington side has a laid-back charm, it's for the waterfalls on the Oregon side of the river that most visitors come to the gorge. The historic Columbia River Highway, between Crown Point and The Dalles, was the brainchild of Washington entrepreneur Sam Hill, who built Maryhill—now a spectacular museum housing Columbia Indian artifacts, Rodin sculptures, and a replica of Stone Henge—in the eastern gorge for his wife Mary. Hill, who made his money on the railroad, interested Portland businessmen John B. Yeon and Simon Benson in improving transportation through the gorge, which up until then had been by steamship or railroad. Opened in 1916, the highway is a stone masterpiece whose stone trestle bridges blend seamlessly with the gorge and make a photogenic foreground to some of the loveliest falls in the country.

The remaining 22-mile segment from 733-foot Crown Point is still the gorge's most popular drive. It passes 38 waterfalls, including Multnomah Falls, the second highest fall in America. More visitors stop at Multnomah Falls and Lodge, donated to the City of Portland by Benson, than anywhere else in the gorge. The lodge is no longer open to overnight guests but a restaurant serves

Lupine, balsamroot, and Mount Hood. PHOTO ©STEVE TERRILL

Latourell Falls, Guy Talbot State Park, Oregon. PHOTO ©TERRY DONNELLY

Tsagaglalal, "She Who Watches", Columbia Hills State Park. PHOTO ©PAT O'HARA

good meals to day travelers, and a mile-long trail climbs to the spectacular cascades and high-country trails beyond. A small information center has information and a bookstore. Other interpretive centers on the Oregon side can be found at Hood River, Cascade Locks, and The Dalles.

From where I sit, I can see the elegant snow cone of 11,239-foot Mount Hood behind Hood River. Halfway through the gorge, poised between the dry east side and wet west side, Hood River's howling winds create the best wind-surfing conditions in the world, a fact not lost on the thousands of board-hounds who flock to the newly hip town each year. Mount Hood is one of the Cascade volcanoes that began to rise out of a 40-million-year-old landscape 4 million years ago. Like Mount St. Helens and Mount Adams on the Washington side, it is a stratovolcano that violently erupted into existence 70,000 years ago.

The large landslide that dammed the river from Cascade Locks to Umatilla, 700 years ago, almost certainly gave rise to the Indian legend of the Bridge of the Gods, said to have come about after Mounts Adams and Hood feuded over lovely Mount St. Helens. Once a treacherous obstacle for river travelers, the cascades disappeared under the impounded waters behind Bonneville Dam in 1938. A toll bridge of the same name links Stevenson and Cascade Locks today.

The forest closes in again as I climb to Hardy Falls, a 50-foot horsetail fall that forms a whitewater chute from the high country to the lowlands through slick volcanic rocks. Monkeyflower, ferns, and mosses live in the spray zone. I sit and write in my journal and allow the white noise of the water to fill my senses, then descend to cross the base of the fall via a sturdy wooden bridge. I stand to one side to let pass two women with walking sticks descending from Hamilton Mountain. Smiling, we all pause to watch the kids I passed earlier. They are now paddling in the shallows, sliding on mossy rocks, and getting completely and utterly soaked, reaping the rewards of their hard climb.

Columbia River Gorge is first and foremost a park for the people, a place where you can escape the city, learn about nature, and enjoy the outdoors. The U.S. Forest Service (charged with overseeing the Columbia River Gorge National Scenic Area) and the 12-person bi-state commission formed to manage the national scenic area, have had many challenges, principal among them trying to balance protection and support of the economy in the gorge with its scenic, natural, and cultural resources. But the sheer enjoyment on the faces of the kids tells its own success story. They called Sam Hill a dreamer, but I think he would be well pleased.

The Rowena Loops on Historic Columbia River Highway. PHOTO ©JEFFREY L. TORRETTA

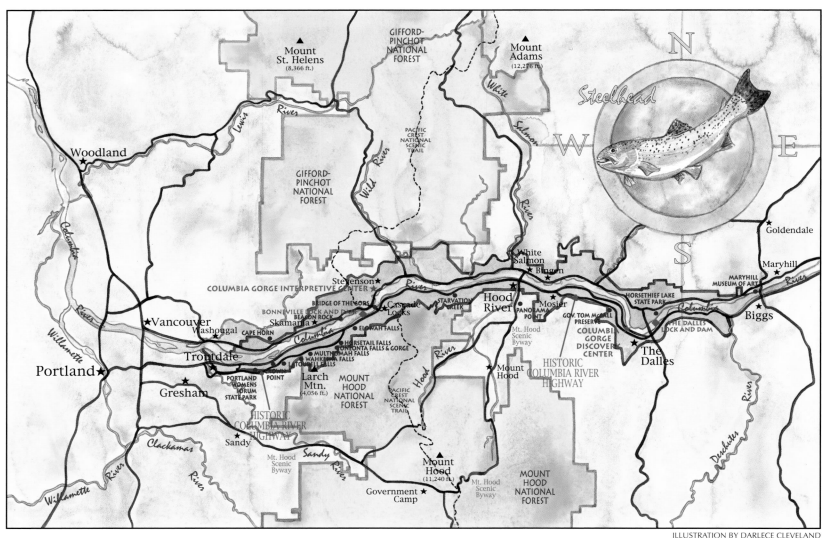

ILLUSTRATION BY DARLECE CLEVELAND

SIZE: 292,500 acres, consisting of 149,400 acres of General Management Areas, 114,600 acres of Special Management Areas, and 28,500 acres of 13 Urban Areas. **FOUNDED:** 1986. **LOCATION:** Columbia River Gorge, spanning the Washington and Oregon sides. Main through-routes are Interstate 84 on the Oregon side and WA 14 on the Washington side. Western access is via US 30 and Interstate 5; eastern access is via US 197 and 97. **HIGHLIGHTS:** Dramatic vistas of the Columbia River, volcanoes, and waterfalls in the surrounding 2,000-4,000-foot volcanic cliffs. Channeled Scablands carved by Ice Age floods 19,000-17,000 years ago. Lewis and Clark National Historical Trail markers. Columbia River People archaeological sites. Historic dams and locks. Rare and endangered plants endemic to the Columbia Gorge. **SEEING THE PARK:** East-west highways on either side of the 80-mile gorge offer access to the main sights. On the Washington side, Highway 14, between Washougal and Wishram, Washington, is quieter although heavily used by logging trucks. Highlights include Bonneville Lock and Dam National Historic Site / Fort Cascades Histori-

cal Trail and The Dalles and John Day Dams; Beacon Rock State Park; Tsagaglalal, "She Who Watches," thought to be a 19th-century Columbia Indian petroglyph at Columbia Hills State Park near Wishram; Maryhill Museum of Art, Goldendale. Oregon highlights include the famous gorge viewpoint at Crown Point; 22-mile Columbia River Historic Highway between Crown Point and Multnomah Falls, and a 9-mile segment between Mosier and The Dalles; Multnomah Falls and Lodge; Bridge of the Gods and Cascade Locks; Hood River and Mount Hood Scenic Byway; Rock Fort, a Lewis and Clark encampment at The Dalles; Deschutes River Crossing, a landmark on the Oregon Trail. **VISITOR CENTERS and MUSEUMS:** (Washington) Skamania Lodge and USFS Interpretive Center and Columbia Gorge Interpretive Center, both in Stevenson; Bonneville Lock and Dam exhibits and fish-counting room; Gorge Heritage Museum, Bingen; Maryhill Museum of Art, Goldendale Observatory Park, and Klickitat County Historical Museum and Presby House in Goldendale; and Columbia Hills State Park petroglyphs, Dallesport. (Oregon) Multnomah

Falls and Lodge Information Center; Hood River County Historical Museum and International Museum of Carousel Art, Hood River; Cascade Locks Historical Museum; Hutson Museum, Parkdale; Columbia Gorge Discovery Center and Wasco County Historical Museum, The Dalles. **CONSIDERATIONS:** Food and lodging are available year round in most of the communities in the Columbia Gorge. Camping and hiking trails are available in state parks and national forests. Riverboat rides are available in Cascade Locks. Gorge roads and trails, and particularly Mount Hood Scenic Byway, may be closed by heavy snow and ice; check conditions before starting out. **CONTACT INFORMATION:** USDA Forest Service, 902 Wasco Avenue, Suite 200, Hood River, OR 97031, (541) 308-1700.

OPPOSITE: Multnomah Falls and footbridge. PHOTO ©JON GNASS

Fort Spokane, Lake Roosevelt N.R.A. PHOTO ©LARRY ULRICH

Officer's Row, Fort Vancouver N.H.S. PHOTO ©STEVE TERRILL

Sherman–Bishop Farm, Ebey's Landing N.H.R.
PHOTO ©MARY LIZ AUSTIN

LAKE ROOSEVELT
NATIONAL RECREATION AREA

Named for the 144-mile-long reservoir backed up behind Grand Coulee Dam in northeast Washington, Lake Roosevelt NRA preserves a large section of the Upper Columbia River for boating, fishing, and other recreation. The area's extraordinary geology (known as the Channeled Scablands) led to the dam's construction in 1932, helping to tame the Columbia River for hydroelectric power, irrigation, and flood control. Three geological provinces meet here—the Okanagan Highlands, Kootenay Arc, and Columbia Plateau—preserving ancient oceanic rocks, volcanic uplifts, and lava flows that built the Plateau. The dam occupies a huge natural gorge, or *coulee*, scoured by catastrophic floods during the last Ice Age. At 550 ft. high, 5,223 ft. long, and containing nearly 12 million cubic yards of concrete, Grand Coulee Dam is the largest concrete structure in North America and the world's third largest producer of hydroelectric power. A visitor center has exhibits, a 13-minute film on the geology of the site and construction of the dam, tours, and popular laser-light shows that use the dam as a backdrop. Camping is available at nearby Steamboat Rock State Park, site of a 2,200-ft-high lava butte in an irrigation reservoir, and Sun Lakes State Park, next to 1,000-ft-high Dry Falls, all that remains of the world's largest waterfall. The Colville Confederated Tribes Museum, in Nespelem, just north of the dam, offers an important counterpoint to Lake Roosevelt. Half on tribal land, the dam has destroyed the enormous annual salmon runs so important to the spiritual identity of the River People. The museum also tells the story of Chief Joseph, the famous Nez Perce chief, who is buried on the reservation.

EBEYS LANDING
NATIONAL HISTORICAL RESERVE

Ebey's Landing on Whidbey Island, at the north end of Puget Sound, was set aside as the nation's first national historic reserve in 1978. A combination of federal, state, county, and private lands, it protects 17,400 acres of beaches, uplands, woods, and prairies; historic pioneer farms homesteaded under the Donation Land Law of 1850; two state parks; and Penn Cove, long used by Skagit Indians from across the Sound. Fort Casey, overlooking the Port Townsend Ferry, is one of three forts built after 1890 to protect Admiralty Inlet, the entrance to Puget Sound, discovered by British captain George Vancouver in 1792. Fort Ebey, built during World War II and named for an early settler, is now crisscrossed by trails that lead to the beach. Coupeville, founded by New England sea captain George Coupe, is the seat of Island County. Many of the 100 historic structures in the reserve can be found on Main Street, a popular location for movie shoots, and home to Island County Historical Museum, a good place to learn more about Central Whidbey Island's history.

FORT VANCOUVER
NATIONAL HISTORIC SITE

Vancouver, on the north bank of the Columbia River, was settled by the powerful British fur-trading Hudson's Bay Company, which, under the guidance of Chief Factor John McLoughlin, built a fort to serve as company administrative headquarters and principal regional supply depot for western America. Known as "the New York of the West," the fort's activities included trade and retail stores, sawmills, grist mills, dairies, tradesmen's shops, agricultural and livestock operations, salmon fisheries, distilleries, and shipbuilding. Hawaiians, French-Canadians, Scots, Irish, American, and members of more than 30 American Indian tribes lived in Kanaka Village near the fort. Business was conducted in French, the main language of canoe-paddling fur-traders ("voyageurs"), and Chinook, the Indian trading language;

English was a distant third. In 1846, the United States began a political takeover on the West Coast, building a fort of their own on the hill above the settlement where famous soldiers such as Sherman and Grant started out their careers. Vancouver Barracks, Officers Row, and the Parade Grounds may still be seen. The 1825 fort has been rebuilt, and may be visited on living history tours with Park Service rangers. All the sites, including the Oregon City house of John McLoughin, are now part of Fort Vancouver National Historic Reserve.

KLONDIKE GOLD RUSH
NATIONAL HISTORICAL PARK

One of the tiniest park service sites in the Lower 48, this redbrick building in Seattle's oldest neighborhood is really a museum, commemorating Seattle's important role as outfitter for prospectors headed for the Klondike goldfields during the 1897-98 gold rush in northwest Canada. The human experience is captured with old photos of grizzled miners, explorers, and early settlers in the Klondike and exhibits of mining paraphernalia. The park offers gold-panning demonstrations, film presentations, and special exhibits throughout the year. Other units of the park are in southeast Alaska.

SAN JUAN ISLAND
NATIONAL HISTORICAL PARK

This park commemorates one of the oddest and most famous incidents in Northwest history. The so-called Pig War over ownership of the San Juan Islands broke out in 1849, triggered by the killing of a British soldier's pig by an American settler. The incident escalated into a full-blown stand-off, with 500 American soldiers up against 2,200 British soldiers and five warships readying for battle. The saber-rattling amounted to nothing, however, and in 1872 the British ceded the territory to the Americans without bloodshed. The park preserves English Camp and American

Camp, on opposite sides of the island. English Camp has a blockhouse, commissary, and barracks, on the north end of Garrison Bay, while American Camp, on the southern end, preserves fortifications and has a visitor center. In summer, you can take guided hikes or watch military reenactments.

WHITMAN MISSION
NATIONAL HISTORIC SITE

This famous historic site near Walla Walla, in southeastern Washington, commemorates Dr. Marcus and Narcissa Whitman, Presbyterian missionaries to the Cayuse Indians in 1836. The first white settlement in this part of the Oregon Country, the Whitman Mission, known as Waiilatpu, or "Place of the People of the Rye Grass," became an important stop on the Oregon Trail. Narcissa Whitman and Eliza Spalding, a neighboring missionary, were the first white women to travel overland on the trail. The mission was strategically located between the Nez Perce and Umatilla tribes, just east of The Dalles, a major trading rendezvous. The Whitmans tried to teach the Cayuse, a nomadic tribe, to farm without success. In 1847, a measles epidemic killed half the Cayuse but spared whites, sparking anger in the tribe. The Whitmans were blamed and subsequently murdered, and 60 other inhabitants—most emigrants—were taken hostage. After John McLoughlin of the Hudson's Bay Company intervened, the hostages were released. The murders prompted Congress to designate Oregon a U.S. territory. The site preserves the foundations of mission buildings, a segment of the Oregon Trail, a graveyard where the victims of the measles epidemic are buried, and the 1897 monument to the Whitmans. There is a museum with exhibits, a slide show, and a bookstore but no food and drink. Rangers offer talks in summer.

Interior, Klondike Gold Rush N.H.P. PHOTO ©TERRY DONNELLY

English Camp, San Juan Island N.H.P. PHOTO ©LARRY ULRICH

Covered wagon, Whitman Mission N.H.S.
PHOTO ©CHARLES GURCHE

Balsamroot, vetch, and Oregon oak. PHOTO ©TERRY DONNELLY

Common camas. PHOTO ©LARRY ULRICH

Moss-covered big-leaf maple. PHOTO ©JOHN MARSHALL

Bunchberry dogwood. PHOTO ©TERRY DONNELLY

The cool, dense forests of the Northwest are a feature of the wet, west side of the mountains. Towering conifers grow to the water's edge, forming a necklace of lowland forests. Arrow-straight Douglas-fir, named for 19th-century Scottish naturalist David Douglas and the most important tree in the logging industry, is easily recognizable. A pioneer species, it is the first to seed in after a disturbance, along with red alder, a smaller-diameter tree favored by Natives in smoking salmon. It is found on both sides of the Cascades and is the dominant tree today in forests on the east side of the Olympic Peninsula, following fires 300 years ago that altered forest succession.

If conditions permit, Douglas-fir can grow over 20 stories tall and live more than 700 years. Before then, it usually yields to shade-tolerant western hemlock, western red cedar, big-leafed maple, and more rarely, Sitka spruce, which favors the tops of seastacks along the coast. Western hemlock grows fast—as tall as 200 feet and 23 feet in circumference—and takes over as a climax species. With its droopy crown, elegant skirted shape, and somber green hue, it captures the moody ambiance of the Northwest and is the state tree.

Deciduous big-leafed maple also sparks the imagination, arrayed in a thick velvet coat of emerald spike moss and wild old-man hair of licorice fern. But the "spirit tree" of the forest is undoubtedly western red cedar, which arrived on these shores as the climate warmed, 6,000 years ago and helped jumpstart Northwest Indian culture. Rot resistant and fragrant, it is still used for buildings, dugout canoes, and in Northwest arts and crafts.

Assertive understory plants like thimbleberry, salal, vine maple, and thorny devil's club dominate the forest floor, hiding white-flowered trillium, oxalis, and smaller woodland neighbors. There's nothing retiring about rhododendron, the state flower. It is one of the most show-stopping flowers in the forest, where it thrives on the acidic soil. That's also true of Pacific dogwood, another species that gives the forest the air of a landscaped garden. Blackberry, huckleberry, salmonberry, and other thorny bushes are beloved by two-legged and four-legged animals such as bears, who fatten up on berries in summer.

Space on the forest floor is at such a premium, tree seedlings frequently germinate in fallen red cedar and other tree trunks that take centuries to rot. The seedlings send down taproots on either side of the "nurse log," creating colonnades of bandy-legged trees. Epiphytes employ a different strategy. These harmless plants wrap themselves around high branches and draw moisture from the air. They contribute tons of biomass to the forest canopy and have become an important part of the Olympic and North Cascade temperate rain forest ecosystem.

THE HIGH COUNTRY

The route to the high country passes through forested drainages. Rain forest changes to predominantly western hemlock and Pacific silver fir at mid-elevation. The appearance of mountain hemlock forests leads the way into a diminishing tree zone characterized primarily by wind-blown dwarf *krummholz*, pruned into tortured shapes by high-altitude winds. Above 3,500 feet, subalpine fir, Pacific silver fir, mountain hemlock, and stands of lodgepole pine and long-living Alaska yellow cedar mark what, this far north, is considered high country.

Lowland forests offer year-round hiking amid generally drizzly conditions—the exception being summer months, from July to September, when the jet stream changes, the skies clear, and temperatures become so warm and dry, drought conditions prevail. That's the time nature-lovers head to the subalpine region, to take advantage of melting snow. Subalpine meadows, such as those found at Hurricane Ridge in Olympic National Park and above Sunrise and Paradise in Mount Rainier National Park, begin at 4,500 feet and are major summer destinations for wildflower viewing.

This is a land isolated by blizzards and deep snowdrifts for eight months of the year, the great timber lodges covered to their rooftops in snow. Spring usually arrives in early June, when melting snow swells waterfalls and rivers. Avalanche and glacier lilies are the first to poke up through snow, then a succession of lupines, asters, red Indian paintbrush, pearly everlasting, pasqueflower, Columbia lilies, and other fast-bloomers arrive, intent on reproducing before the snows return.

Plants living higher up in the alpine zone have made remarkable adaptations to the cold, wind-drying conditions. Moss campion, Tolmie's saxifrage, and alpine phlox have woody stems, grow in mats low to the ground, and hide from the wind behind scattered stones, or fellfields. Among them, heather, which forms lavender-colored sprays, is remarkably long-lived—pollen dating has suggested that some of Mount Rainier's heathers have been here 7,000 years—but is easily trampled. Watch where you walk. The high country is home to a number of endemic species, among them Flett's violet and Piper's bellflower, both pretty flowers only found in the Olympics.

EAST MEETS WEST
Columbia River Gorge, which spans both east and west sides of the Cascades, is one of the most botanically diverse areas in the Northwest, home to more than 1,000 species of wildflower. Sixteen plants are endemic, and 58 are endangered or threatened species, including Barrett's penstemon and bitterroot. Riverbanks offer a moist environment for black cottonwood, willow, red alder, and Oregon ash, as well as prairie camas, a nutri-

tious dietary staple. Lowland forests of red cedar, Douglas fir, and western hemlock and waterfall margins harbor spring truffles and monkeyflower, bleedingheart, and rain-lovers such as *Romanzoffia sitchensis*, found only in Oneonta Gorge.

Dry hills dotted with Oregon white oak and marshy ponds filled with rushes can be seen at The Nature Conservancy's Tom McCall Preserve on Rowena Plateau, east of Mosier. Here is a changing show of grass widow, spring-lily, balsamroot, desert parsley, and others. Look east from here to the Channeled Scabland terraces for golden grasses and big sagebrush as far as the eye can see, as well as the occasional bitterroot, a traditional medicine. The desert is closer than you think in dry rain-shadow areas like the eastern Cascades and the San Juans, where you'll encounter pricklypear cactus and juniper trees more commonly found in the Southwest.

Englemann spruce, western larch, and quaking aspen begin in the high country—6,500 feet on the dry side of the Cascades. At lower elevations, the indicator species are Douglas-fir and ponderosa pine, both trees valued for lumber. Ponderosas grow in tall, airy stands and have a wonderful thick, tannin-rich bark that smells of vanilla. A century of fire suppression has transformed many forests into doghair thickets of young trees surrounded by thick duff that fuel destructive crown fires.

Sub-alpine fir. PHOTO ©FRED HIRSCHMANN

Avalanche lily. PHOTO ©RICHARD D. STRANGE

Old-growth western hemlocks. PHOTO ©TERRY DONNELLY

Vanilla leaf and fir. PHOTO ©JOHN MARSHALL

Osprey in flight. PHOTO ©TIM FITZHARRIS

Mountain goat. PHOTO ©CRAIG BLACKLOCK/LARRY ULRICH STOCK

Olympic marmot. PHOTO ©ROB TILLEY

Roosevelt elk in Hoh Rain Forest. PHOTO ©ART WOLFE

Washington's forests may seem cathedral quiet but there is a wealth of wildlife there. Chattering in the branches are squirrels, which harvest nuts and descend to dig for mycorrhizae, or fungi, growing on tree roots, an activity that improves the nitrogen content of the poor, acidic soil. Pine martens, a relative of the weasel, have lived in Northwest forests since glacial times. Columbia black-tailed deer wander through the understory and provide prey for cougars, which may travel hundreds of miles daily to obtain food but are rarely seen.

In Olympic's Hoh Rain Forest, look in the mud for the hoofprints of Roosevelt elk. These large mammals aggressively prune young trees and help keep the growth under control. In the wettest areas, you'll also see the silvery mucous trail of slugs, which require 100 percent humidity to avoid drying out. The spooky-looking banana slug is the largest of 23 species on the Olympic Peninsula. The Pacific giant salamander also likes wet areas. It is the largest of 18 species found on the peninsula.

Old-growth forests in Olympic and Mount Rainier National Parks are important refuges for two endangered bird species. Northern spotted owls, fifth largest of the 19 owl species, nest in tree cavities deep in the forest. Without waterproof wings, the birds rely on the thick canopy to keep dry and shield young birds feeding on the forest floor from predators. Marbled murrelets are even more secretive. They nest in forests as far away as Mount Rainier and return daily to the coast, up to 50 miles away, to fish for food for their young. The state bird, the cheery American goldfinch, can often be seen eating seeds from thistles late in the summer, its song a beautiful trill in grassy areas throughout Washington.

COASTS AND WETLANDS

The Olympic coastline provides important habitat for animals of sea, land, and air. Washington Islands Wilderness Area spans 100 miles and has 870 rocks, reefs, and islands used by thousands of birds. Protection Island, in the Strait of Juan de Fuca, is now a national wildlife refuge for 60,000 seabirds, among them 30 species, including cormorants, pigeon guillemots, black oyster-catchers, tufted puffins, rhinocerous auklets, and murres. More than a million western sandpipers are among 24 species that feed in the rich tidal flats of Gray's Harbor estuary on the peninsula. In Hood Canal and other tidal areas, geoducks, or razor clams, oysters, and Dungeness crabs have been harvested for millennia. Occasional "red tides," or algae blooms, make collection dangerous at times. Check before you dig.

The Cape Flattery area is one of the best places in North America to see large numbers of hawks. Other birds of prey congregate on San Juan Island, which has populations of goshawks, dusky horned owls, Cooper's hawks, and bald eagles. Once endangered bald eagles have made a comeback and are most visible at Skagit River Bald Eagle Natural Area on the North Cascades Highway, where they dine on chum salmon in winter. They also nest in Discovery Park, a large urban park overlooking Puget Sound in Seattle. Birds of prey can also be seen on lamp posts and snags around Lake Washington, where wetlands such as those at Mercer Slough are gathering places for red-winged blackbirds and other riparian species.

Tide pools, exposed at low tide, can contain 4,000 creatures per square foot. Among them are colorful kelp, mussels, urchins, anemones, crabs, whelks, and an astonishing 40 species of sea stars. The latter prey on their poolmates, and in turn are delicacies for glaucous-winged gulls, crows, raccoons, bears, and other beachcombers. The huge offshore kelp beds offer resting places for sea otters, Pacific harbor seals, and migrating gray whales, which have now rebounded from their endangered species status.

High spots along the coast at Kalaloch and in Oregon are best for watching gray whales migrate from Alaska to their breeding grounds in Baja California in December and January. In 1999, the Makah tribe, headquartered near Cape Flattery, returned to ceremonial canoe hunting of up to five gray whales a year, part of an important cultural renaissance in the tribe. Resident and transient pods of orcas, or killer whales, living in the Strait of Juan de Fuca around the San Juan Island are faring much worse, probably due to disturbance from whale-watching cruises and polluted salmon on which they feed.

Six native species of Northwest salmon—chinook or king, coho or silver, chum or dog, steelhead, humpback or pink, and sockeye or red—on Olympic, Cascade, and Columbia rivers are now endangered in Washington, after dam building, logging, overfishing, pollution, and manmade development destroyed runs that once numbered in their millions. Fish ladders, filters to protect the fish from turbines, and barge and truck transport of young smolts around dams have done little to improve the situation. Salmon, anadromous species that return from several years of growth at sea to spawn in the rivers, streams, and lakes, seem destined to die out without the political will to save them.

HIGH COUNTRY REFUGES

On the Olympic Peninsula, there is an extraordinary level of endemism among both plant and animal species, most likely due to isolation during the Ice Age, which stranded populations in high-country refugia. Olympic has unique species of marmot, snow

mole, chipmunk, pocket gopher, and Beardslee and Crescenti trout. Black bear, cougar, Columbia black-tailed deer, and Roosevelt elk, live elsewhere. Red foxes and mountain goats were introduced. The Olympic ecosystem is intact, except for endangered gray wolves, which prey on elk and deer.

You won't find grizzly bear and lynx on the Olympic Peninsula, but they do live—albeit out of sight—in the North Cascades, an enormous mountain park contiguous with wildlands in British Columbia. Among the charismatic species you may glimpse are mountain goats. These goats sport a long, warm coat and have flexible cloven hoofs that allow them access to the highest mountainsides in the Cascades and the remote Selkirk Mountains of northeastern Washington.

Black bear, which hibernate and give birth to their young in the den, are frequently sighted in high-country forests and meadows in late summer fattening up on tender tree shoots, berries, and salmon dying in streams after spawning. In Washington, they may be black, brown, or cinnamon-hued.

Perhaps the most unusual high-country species is one that is almost impossible to see. The inch-long ice worm lives in glaciers on the slopes of Mount Rainier, Mount Olympus, and other peaks. They are largely nocturnal (except on Mount Rainier) eat snow fleas, pollen grains, fern spores, and algae that blow onto the glaciers on the winds. Ravens and rosy finches feed on these worms.

Saw-whet owlet. PHOTO ©ART WOLFE

Bald eagle. PHOTO ©MARK & JENNIFER MILLER

Harbor seals. PHOTO ©ART WOLFE

Seastars and anemones. PHOTO ©PAT O'HARA

PAGE 60/61: Dawn from Columbia Hills State Park, WA, Columbia River Gorge National Scenic Area. PHOTO ©JEFFREY L. TORRETTA

RESOURCES and INFORMATION

IN CASE OF EMERGENCY

Emergency & Medical
Call 911

FOR MORE INFORMATION

Northwest Interpretive Association
(877) 874-6775
www.nwpubliclands.com
Washington's National Park Fund
(206) 770-0627
www.wnpf.org

OTHER REGIONAL SITES

**Ebey's Landing
National Historical Site**
PO Box 774
162 Cemetery Road
Coupeville, WA 98239
(360) 678-6084
www.nps.gov/ebla

**Fort Vancouver
National Historic Site**
612 E. Reserve Street
Vancouver, WA 98661
(360) 696-7655x10
www.nps.gov/fova

**Klondike Gold Rush
National Historical Park**
(Seattle Unit)
319 Second Street South
Seattle, WA 98104
(206) 220-4240
www.nps.gov/klse

**Lake Roosevelt
National Recreation Area**
1008 Crest Drive
Coulee Dam, WA 99116
(509) 633-9441
www.nps.gov/laro

Mount Rainier National Park
55210 238th Avenue East
Ashford, WA 98304
E-mail: MORAInfo@nps.gov
(360) 569-2211
(360) 569-2177 (TDD)
www.nps.gov/mora

Lewis and Clark National Historical Park
92343 Fort Clatsop Road
Astoria, OR 97103
(503) 861-4408x214
www.nps.gov/lewi

North Cascades National Park Service Complex
Includes:
–North Cascades National Park
810 State Route 20
Sedro-Woolley, WA 98284
(360) 856-5700
www.nps.gov/noca

–Lake Chelan National Recreation Area
c/o North Cascades National Park
810 State Route 20
Sedro-Woolley, WA 98284
(360) 856-5700
www.nps.gov/noca
–Ross Lake National Recreation Area
c/o North Cascades National Park
810 State Route 20

Sedro-Woolley, WA 98284
(360) 856-5700
www.nps.gov/noca
Olympic National Park
600 East Park Avenue
Port Angeles, WA 98362
(360) 565-3130
www.nps.gov/olym

San Juan Island National Historical Park
PO Box 429
Friday Harbor, WA 98250
(360) 378-2902
www.nps.gov/sajh

Whitman Mission National Historic Site
328 Whitman Mission Road
Walla Walla, WA 99362
(509) 522-6357
www.nps.gov/whmi

NATIONAL FOREST INFORMATION

Columbia River Gorge National Scenic Area
902 Wasco Street, Suite 200
Hood River, OR 97031
(541) 386-2333
www.fs.fed.us/r6/columbia/forest

Colville National Forest
765 South Main Street
Colville, WA 99114
(509) 684-7000
www.fs.fed.us/r6/colville

Gifford Pinchot National Forest
10600 NE 51st Circle
Vancouver, WA 98682
(360) 891-5000
www.fs.fed.us/gpnf

Mount Baker–Snoqualmie National Forest
21905 64th Avenue W
Mountlake Terrace, WA 98043
(425) 775-9702
www.fs.fed.us/r6/mbs

Mount Hood National Forest
16400 Champion Way
Sandy, OR 97055
(503) 668-1700
www.fs.fed.us/r6/mthood

Mount St. Helens National Volcanic Monument
Monument Headquarters
42218 NE Yale Bridge Road
Amboy, WA 98601
(360) 449-7800
—or—
Mount St. Helens Visitor Center
3029 Spirit Lake Highway
Castle Rock, WA 98611
(360) 274-0962

Okanogan National Forest
215 Melody Lane
Wenatchee, WA 98801
(509) 664-9200
www.fs.fed.us/r6/oka

Wenatchee National Forest
215 Melody Lane
Wenatchee, WA 98801
(509) 664-9200
www.fs.fed.us/r6/wenatchee

ABOVE: Old-growth forest in morning fog, North Cascades National Park.
PHOTO ©CHARLES GURCHE

OPPOSITE: Old-growth hemlock forest, Upper Sol Duc Valley, Olympic National Park.
PHOTO ©MARY LIZ AUSTIN

ACKNOWLEDGMENTS

Much gratitude to all those in the Northwest park system who took time out of extraordinarily busy summer schedules to assist me in writing this book. Special kudos to Tim Manns at North Cascades National Park Service Complex; Lee Taylor and Sandi Kinzer at Mount Rainier National Park; Kathy Steichen and Margaret Baker at Olympic National Park; Pat Berry at Columbia River Gorge National Scenic Area; Todd Cullings and Steve Rieck at Mount St. Helens National Volcanic Monument; Jim Adams at Northwest Interpretive Association; and Ron Warfield, former Assistant Chief of Interpretation at Mount Rainier National Park. To ex-Northwesterner Cindy Bohn, thanks again for meeting me on the page and doing a great editing job. Additional thanks to Ann Marie Stillion and Eleanor Inskip for shelter from the storm during my travels; to fellow editor Sherri Schultz, always a voice of reason; and to fellow writer and desert refugee Larry Cheek: I'll catch you next time on the trail. Lastly, another round of thanks to Jeff Nicholas, whose generosity of spirit, enduring eye for beauty, and concern for our public lands are a fine match for the inspiring natural and cultural history to be found in America's national parks.

—N.L.

The publisher would like to take this opportunity to extend his heartfelt thanks to Northwest Interpretive Associations Executive Director: Jim Adams and his extraordinary staff members: David Ranck, Sue Kirk, Lori Herr, Margaret Baker, and Lana Kidner for their assistance in making this publication as accurate and up-to-date as possible. Many Thanks!   J.D.N.

PRODUCTION CREDITS

Publisher: Jeff D. Nicholas
Author: Nicky Leach
Editor: Cindy Bohn
Illustrations: Darlece Cleveland
Printing Coordination: Sung In Printing America

ISBN 10: 1-58071-068-9 (Paper)
ISBN 13: 978-1-58071-068-8 (Paper)

SIERRA PRESS
4988 Gold Leaf Drive, Mariposa, CA 95338
(800) 745-2631, e-mail: siepress@sti.net
www.NationalParksUSA.com

ABOVE
Mount Rainier and Spirit Lake visible above the rim of Mount St. Helens. PHOTO ©TYSON FISHER
OPPOSITE
Sunset from Hurricane Ridge, Olympic National Park. PHOTO ©PAT O'HARA